IDAHO MOUNTAIN RANGES

BY GEORGE WUERTHNER

NUMBER ONE

© copyright 1986 by
AMERICAN GEOGRAPHIC PUBLISHING
HELENA, MONTANA 59604
All rights reserved

RICK GRAETZ, PUBLISHER
MARK THOMPSON, DIRECTOR OF PUBLICATIONS
BARBARA FIFER, ASSISTANT BOOK EDITOR

This series provides in-depth information about Idaho geographical, natural history, historical and cultural subjects. Design by Len Visual Design. Printed in Japan by DNP America, Inc., San Francisco.

Writing a book about a subject as broad as Idaho's mountains inevitably means leaving out a great deal of interesting material. It also means that I could not include every mountain area in the state, though I have tried to write about major, representative ranges in each sub-region. If you live in Council by the Cuddy Mountains or outside of Malta near the Jim Sage Mountains or by any of the smaller ranges which I had to exclude from the text, please forgive me. These omission were not due to carelessness, but result from the constraints imposed by the text limitations.

Space limitations also made it necessary to generalize about the appearance of particular mountains, climate, land uses, elevation and other descriptive terms. Hence while a particular mountain range may well have some rugged cliffs or individual peaks, if it had an overall rolling nature, I described it as such. The same for other variable features.

Nearly all of Idaho's mountain ranges are under some public ownership and management. As a consequence, I dwelled on a number of management issues including the question of wilderness designation. As with any other issue, there are many viewpoints and there is no agreement on which areas or how much acreage should be preserved as wilderness within the state. The boundaries and acreage proposed constantly change and as a result the figures used in the text should be viewed as guidelines, not absolutes. Depending upon the philosophies of the group considering the wilderness issue, the acreage of each wilderness proposal may vary from zero to hundreds of thousands of acres. I have usually provided only the greater figure so readers would have a general idea of the unit's potential size and have included acreage from Montana where proposals cross state lines. Figures also may vary because of boundary adjustments. Some groups propose combining sev eral ranges into one complete unit, while others may propose separate wildernesses for each individual mountain mass. For example, in the White Cloud Peaks region, the state's Congressional delegation proposes wilderness classification of the White Cloud Mountains, but none for surrounding ranges, while at the other extreme there are several conservation groups advocating wilderness designation for a combined White Cloud, Boulder and Pioneer Mountains area, including both

Sunset along the Lost River Range. GEORGE WUERTHNER

Forest Service and BLM roadless lands.

The same qualification applies to current environmental issues such as forest planning, grazing plans and other controversial land management policies. Many of the forest plans are being appealed and, as a consequence, changes may occur that could alter some numbers in the book, such as the extent of roading, the profitability of grazing fees, or the amount of administratively endorsed wilderness. Nevertheless, in most cases the general trends remain the same. In addition, various analyses of the same issue may arrive at different results due to variations in the specific data used. For example, a recent review of National Forest timber sales by the Wilderness Society and the Idaho Conservation League concluded that, as a rule, Idaho's National Forests lose money on their timber sales. Each group used different methods to evaluate these sales and, not surprisingly, their numbers do not agree, but both conclude that timber harvest is not profitable on much of Idaho's timberlands.

Although it should be obvious to the reader that I support wilderness designation for Idaho's roadless country, it should be remembered that the vast majority of Idaho's public lands and mountains ranges are devoted primarily to other uses, including grazing, timber harvest, mining and other resource development. In most cases, these activities are legitimate uses of the land and should be continued. If I appear to be critical of timber harvest, it is not that I oppose the cutting of trees, but often only how the forest is exploited and where. It is not in the long-term interest of Idahoans or the nation to have small, slow-growing trees cut on steep, highly erodable slopes that will impact fisheries, wildlife and other forest resources, and this careless resource exploitation attempted to bring to the reader's attention. The same can be said for other uses. Overgrazing is not in the best interest of the public or the rancher.

While it's entirely appropriate to exploit some of the public land, Idaho also has some of the wildest large tracts of roadless country left in the nation. It is a resource value that cannot be recreated and one that can only be lost. Any action with non-reversible consequences should be thoughtfully evaluated and I hope this book will contribute to that end.

GEORGE WUERTHNER

CONTENTS

ISBN 0-938314-26-2

Published by American Geographic Publishing
Idaho-Montana-Oregon-Washington-Wyoming
Box 5630, Helena, Montana 59604   (406) 443-2842

Front cover photos
Left: Blue camas, Packer's Meadow, Clearwater
National Forest. GEORGE WUERTHNER
Top: Mt. Regan, Sawtooth Lake. JEFF GNASS
Center: Bull elk. HARRY JARVIS
Lower right: Atop the Bitterroot Divide above Goose
Creek. GEORGE WUERTHNER
Inset: Columbine. BRUCE SELYEM
This page, left: Cow Creek, Selkirk Mountains.
JOANNE PAVIA

The Sawtooths are Idaho's best-known range. They form a serrated skyline in this view near Stanley.
GEORGE WUERTHNER

On the wall above my desk is a map of Idaho. If I use my imagination the general outline of the state looks something like a human footprint in wet sand with the northern panhandle as the heel, the Bitterroot Divide forming the insole, and the big toe lying in the southeast corner near where Idaho joins Wyoming and Utah.

The northern panhandle or heel of my imaginary foot is less than forty miles wide, while down in the south where the toes would lie, the state broadens to 300 miles in width. It is a direct line east to west from the Wyoming border to the Oregon border with both Utah and Nevada to the south. The outside edge of the foot, bounded as it is by Oregon and Washington, is more or less a 480-mile straight line, except for a few squiggles where the Snake River intercedes as the boundary between Oregon and Idaho.

Within these bounds are 82,677 square miles—an area larger than New York, New Jersey, New Hampshire, and Massachusetts combined, and approximately the same size as Great Britain—yet there are fewer than a million residents. The largest city, Boise, with 102,000 people, would barely qualify as a population center back east. Even as western cities go, it is rather small. There is no equivalent of Denver, Phoenix, or even a moderate-sized Salt Lake City in Idaho. Instead the state's population is spread out in a number of modest-sized communities that are strung along southern Idaho's Snake River.

The names of Idaho cities located along the Snake River and its tributaries sound like a roll call of nearly all the state's major urban areas. There is Rexburg, followed by Idaho Falls, Blackfoot, Pocatello, American Falls, Burley, Twin Falls, Boise, Nampa, Caldwell, Payette, and finally Weiser where the Snake enters Hells Canyon. Some of these cities are tucked up against hills or peaks. Pocatello, for example, sits on the edge of the mountains, with only one flank exposed to the flat lands; others such as Twin Falls spill out across the plain with no mountains to restrict or define growth. But whether an Idaho city is on the plain or huddled up against the hills, you can always see mountains in some direction, sometimes in all directions. Of all the states in the Rockies, none is more mountainous than Idaho, but unlike neighboring Montana, which has large cities like Missoula, Helena and Bozeman within its intermontane valleys, most Idahoans do not live in the mountains. Instead, they live up against the hills, but looking out toward the open spaces.

Statistics tell the story. There are 81 named ranges within the state—give or take a few depending upon which map you consult. The highest point is Mt. Borah at 12,662'; the low of 738' lies near Lewiston where the Snake River leaves the state. In between these two elevations, there are mountains and hills covering the entire state except for the Snake River Plain and some larger valleys and prairies between ranges. More than half the state is between 5,000' and 10,000' in elevation, with over 200 named peaks exceeding 8,000' in elevation. The criterion "named" is important, for there are numerous summits, some over 12,000', that lack a formal name.

Idaho's mountains can be divided into several sub-regions based on similarities in geology, climate, terrain and plant cover. The mountains of northern Idaho are low compared to those ranges farther south; none of the peaks exceeds 8,000'. Rainfall is high and forest cover extensive and dense. Along the Canadian border are the glacier-carved Selkirk and Purcell mountains. Farther south one runs into the low rolling ridges of the Coeur d'Alene and St. Joe.

In the mid-section of the state lie the mountains of the huge Idaho Batholith—a massive plateau-like outcrop of granite deeply dissected by tumultuous rivers like the Salmon and Selway. Few roads penetrate this region and only one paved road, Highway 12, crosses

5

it. South of that road on this central portion of my map there are no red lines symbolizing paved highways; none exists. This is Idaho's wilderness core, where one must still hike or pack to cross ranges like the Bitterroots and Salmon River Mountains.

South and east of the towns of Challis and Salmon, the mountains separate into more distinct ranges with definite valleys between them—what are often called the Broad Valley Rockies. Small towns like Leadore and Mackay hunker down in the valley floors, almost swallowed up by the vastness of the landscape, dwarfed by the towering summits of Idaho's highest peaks in the Lemhi, Lost River and Pioneer Mountains. An arid climate restricts tree growth to the highest ridges and north-facing slopes; grasses dominate the lower elevations and drier exposures. The lack of forest cover makes these peaks appear even higher and more rugged, for there is nothing to soften the jagged edge of rock or interfere with the sweeping vistas.

Farther west near McCall and extending south to Boise are the rolling granite ridges and peaks that comprise the Payette Crest, Boise Mountains and other ranges generally lacking accepted formal names. All these mountains are outcrops of the Idaho Batholith, and appear as a crumpled, dissected mass of hills and peaks with few distinct boundaries separating one range from the next.

South of these ranges and the mountains of the Broad Valley Rockies, the lava flows of the Snake River Plain have flooded the southern third of the state. Beyond Twin Falls and Burley near the Utah border are some outlying mountains of the Basin and Range province: the Black Pine, Albion, Cassia and others. As is typical of the Basin and Range, wide, dry valleys separate these rock outcrops into isolated ranges.

These Basin and Range mountains continue eastward toward the Wyoming border where they blend into ranges considered part of the Middle Rockies. There is no clear-cut boundary between one geographical province and the

Jack's Creek has cut this canyon in the basalt plateau of the Owyhee Mountains. GEORGE WUERTHNER

next, but the Caribou, Snake River and Aspen ranges are generally viewed as part of the Middle Rockies. Other ranges such as the Bannock Range are often placed in either category, and I have made the split just west of this range. These southeastern Idaho mountain ranges such as the Caribou, Snake River, Bear River and others are all part of the oil-bearing Overthrust Belt. Taken as a region, these southeastern mountains are wetter and more heavily forested than either the Broad Valley Rockies or the mountains of the Basin and Range province.

The remaining mountainous area of the state lies in the southwest near the Oregon-Nevada border, where the Owyhee Mountains rise out of the Snake River Plain lowlands. This is Idaho's least known and most isolated mountain area, the entire region of canyons, hills and mountains called the "Owyhee Country."

Nearly all of Idaho's major mountain ranges are public domain. Bureau of Land Management (BLM) and Forest Service lands, plus other federal land holdings, make up 65 percent of the state—second only to Nevada in percentage of public land among the western states. Of Idaho's 53 million total acres, more than a third—some 20,351,874 acres—are managed by the U.S. Forest Service. Another 12,113,193 acres are controlled by the BLM, and 2.5 million are divided up among other federal agencies. Only 19,106,505 acres of Idaho are privately owned. While some Idahoans say this large amount of federal ownership hinders the state's economic growth, it is interesting to note that California is nearly 50 percent federally owned, but nevertheless manages to maintain a robust economy.

Most of Idaho's mountains have some forest cover and Idaho's 21.6 million acres of forest lands give it the distinction of being the most heavily timbered of the Rocky Mountain states. Still, compared to other states, Idaho's forested acres are not unusual. For example, Georgia has 25 million acres of forest lands, and densely populated California has even more timberland, with 40,152,000 tree-covered acres. Nevertheless, in the arid west, where sagebrush is more common than a tree, Idaho's forestlands are a substantial asset.

In the wetter northern mountains of the state where precipitation can exceed 90 inches a year, the timber industry dominates the economy of many communities. Vast forests of white pine, western red cedar, western hemlock, western larch and Douglas fir reminiscent of the Pacific Northwest blanket northern Idaho, although many of the lower-elevation timber stands have been cut.

As one moves southward in the state, annual precipitation falls off and plant communities adapted to arid climates prevail, at least at lower elevations. Grasses, and scrubs like sagebrush, dominate the mountain slopes. Trees are restricted to the waterways and the higher, wetter basins and slopes. Livestock grazing replaces logging as the main economic entity, so that southern Idaho's mountains are the domain of the rancher.

In the past, Idaho's mountains were considered a barrier to progress and an economic liability. It was difficult to farm the narrow mountain valleys and many of them were too high and cold for successful agriculture. The rugged terrain made logging expensive and difficult. Even livestock, if given a choice, avoid grazing steep, hilly country. If you undertook one of these endeavors, getting your product to market was hampered by a lack of roads and highways. The transportation network of highways and railroads through the high passes and along winding river valleys was expensive to construct and difficult to maintain. Yet these very same rugged, isolated mountains make Idaho attractive for a wide variety of outdoor recreational activities including fishing, hunting, river running, skiing, camping and backpacking. Tourism and outdoor recreation are rapidly becoming important to local economies that once were almost entirely dependent upon industries such as logging or ranching. Over four million people visit the state each year, making the travel industry Idaho's third largest economic producer, generating over $1 billion of income.

Several areas of the state have been given special recognition for their unique wild beauty, including the Sawtooth National Recreation Area, Hells Canyon Wilderness, Frank Church/River of No Return Wilderness, Selway-Bitterroot Wilderness, Gospel Hump Wilderness and the Craters of the Moon National Monument. Flowing from the mountains are a number of federally designated Wild and Scenic Rivers, including the Selway, Middle Fork of the Salmon, Main Salmon, Snake, Middle Fork of the Clearwater and Lochsa. Additional Idaho rivers presently under study

The Lochsa River, which drains the Bitterroot Mountains, is one of Idaho's several Wild and Scenic Rivers. More than 4 million tourists a year visit these rivers, contributing more than a billion dollars to the state's income. GEORGE WUERTHNER

for Wild and Scenic River status include the Henry's Fork, Priest, Falls, Bruneau, Owyhee, Jarbidge and portions of the Snake.

In spite of nearly a century of logging and mining, nearly 10 million acres of the state's national Forest Service lands are still roadless, but not included within a designated wilderness. In addition, millions of acres of BLM lands currently are under study as potential additions to the wilderness system. No other state, outside of Alaska, has such vast holdings of potential and designated wild, roadless country.

Debate upon which of these areas, if any, should be added to the National Wilderness Preservation System has been long and heated. For the most part, the Idaho Congressional delegation is opposed to any new wilderness within the state. In 1984 they introduced a bill calling for the addition of 550,000 acres to the wilderness system in Idaho. Other proposals from the governor, the timber industry and conservation groups recommended wilderness designation for from 750,000 acres to that of all 10 million roadless areas.

With a growing tourist industry dependent upon the state's mountain scenery, wildlife and recreational opportunities, Idaho's mountains will no doubt become appreciated as the state's most important natural resource.

2 GEOLOGY

Many forces, including volcanism, have shaped Idaho's mountains. Here at Craters of the Moon, recent basalt flows pooled against the nearby mountains. JEFF GNASS

A cursory glance at any world atlas shows that mountains do not occur randomly; they are aligned in distinct belts, one of which passes through the western United States. Most geologists believe the theory of plate tectonics explains the occurrence of these mountain belts and offers insight into their origins. According to tectonic theory the earth's crust is a series of moveable plates, many as large as continents, which glide over the more plastic rocks of the mantle, and occasionally collide into one another. One of these plates, the North American plate, has been gradually shifting westward, overriding the eastern edge of the Pacific plate in the process. The stresses of this collision have buckled the earth's surface into mountains in Idaho and throughout the west.

The geology of Idaho's mountains results from these past movements of continental plates. For example, the oldest exposed rocks in Idaho, the Belt Supergroup, were lain down during the Precambrian era some 2 billion years ago, when what is now Idaho was a shallow sea along the margin of an ancient continental plate. Most of these Belt rocks have been metamorphosed (restructured by heat and pressure), but not enough to alter some obvious clues to their origins. Ripple marks, mud cracks and raindrops still show that these sediments were washed into shallow seas, which periodically retreated to create such features. At some later date, the plate upon which these Belt rocks formed broke up and eventually became part of newer continental plates. Today, rocks very similar to the Belt rocks of north Idaho can also be seen in Siberia and China. They are assumed to be widely dispersed remnants of the same ancient plate.

At a much later date, during the Paleozoic era, some 600 to 225 million years ago (about the time fishes first evolved), marine sediments were deposited over much of southern

Idaho. The limestones that make up parts of the Lost River Range, Bear River Range and the Beaverhead Mountains, as well as other central and southern Idaho mountains, and the Phosphora formation that comprises the great phosphate belt extending from Montana south through Idaho and Wyoming, were all formed while these ancient seas covered the region.

In the later part of this era, what is now the North American plate was united with other continental plates to form a huge super-continent centered in the southern hemisphere. The land mass that became North America was then much closer to the equator and farther east than at present. Approximately 200 million years ago, this predecessor of the North American plate, along with the plates that would one day be Europe and Asia, broke away from the super-continent. About 100 to 80 million years ago, a further split occurred and North America separated from the other two continental masses and began to drift westward.

As this plate overrode the Pacific Plate, the

Many central and northern Idaho mountains are composed of Idaho Batholith granite, as seen here in outcrops along the Middle Fork of the Boise River, on the southern edge of the batholith. Above left: Whitebark pine struggles for existence in granites of the Idaho batholith in the Bitterroot Mountains.
GEORGE WUERTHNER PHOTOS

9

The glaciated, U-shaped valley of the North Fork of the Big Lost River in the Boulders. Color variations in vegetation to the right of the present channel hint at paths of previous channels. GEORGE WUERTHNER

earth's crust was driven deep under the continental margin into what is called a subduction zone, where the rocks melt and become magma. Magma is lighter than the surrounding rocks, so tends to rise toward the earth's surface and occasionally flows out as volcanic eruptions. (The line of volcanoes along the Cascade Range marks an active subduction zone where the eastward-moving Pacific plate has been overridden by the westbound North American plate.) In many cases the liquid rock fails to reach the surface and cools in place under the crust, forming granitic rocks. In Idaho, the subduction zone along the leading edge of the westward-moving North American plate formed magma that eventually cooled to create the giant granitic body known as the Idaho Batholith. Other Idaho batholiths such as the Kanuksu and Owyhee were emplaced about this same time. As the North American plate continued its slow westward slide, the zone of active magma formation gradually shifted

eastward. Thus, the oldest parts of the Idaho Batholith, along the western edge, are some 90 million years old, while the youngest granites, some 60 million years in age, make up the eastern edge near the Idaho-Montana border.

Eventually the overlying rocks that covered the batholiths were eroded away, exposing the granite. Granites are very hard rocks and resistant to weathering; hence, as softer rock materials are stripped away, the granite core remains and forms the backbone of many of the world's dramatic mountain ranges. The Teton, Sierra Nevada, Wind River and Himalaya mountains, among others, are made wholly or in part of exposed granite cores. In Idaho the mountain ranges that are partially or predominantly composed of granitic batholiths include the Selkirk, Owyhee, Cabinet, Bitterroot, Salmon River, Sawtooth, Payette Crest, Boise and Clearwater mountains.

Mineralization is common around batholiths and many of the early gold and silver mining

discoveries of Idaho were located along the edge of the Idaho Batholith and other granitic bodies. It is thought that the tremendous heat associated with the rising magma, in combination with water, dissolves minerals into solution, concentrating them from the surrounding rock. Then, as the solution cools or the water is driven off, the minerals are precipitated out, forming veins and lode deposits. The association of gold discoveries with batholiths is so pronounced that one can almost outline the Idaho Batholith simply by mapping the location of the early placer and lode discoveries.

The rocks of western Idaho adjoining the granite rocks of Idaho's batholiths are of an entirely different structure and origin. They are thought to be islands or small fragments of other continental plates which were jammed onto the western margin of the North American plate approximately 100 million years ago.

Approximately 79 million years ago, about the same time as the emplacement of Idaho's major batholiths, the pressure from the collision of plate fragments and subduction caused crumpling and compression of rock formations in a broad arc from Alberta to Utah. This massive movement of the earth's crust is known as the Overthrust Belt. In the Overthrust Belt of southeast Idaho, older rock formations have been pushed some 35 to 40 miles eastward over younger rocks. These great slabs of the earth's crust were stacked on edge like a pile of lumber, each layer tilted gently to the east, with the harder, more resistant layers remaining as ridges, while the intervening softer sediments have eroded into valleys. This ridge and valley formation is very common in the Caribou, Aspen and other ranges of southeast Idaho. Underneath these rock formations, oil and gas deposits have been trapped, and hence much exploration activity concentrates on this area of the state.

After formation of the batholiths, as well as the development of overthrust belts 60 million years ago, the compression and folding ended and, geologically, things were quiet for a while. Then, some 50 million years ago, volcanic eruptions blanketed central Idaho, forming the highly colored and erosive rocks known as the Challis Volcanics. The Challis Volcanics are common in the White Knob, Salmon River, Lemhi, Beaverhead and Lost River ranges—all near the town of Challis, for which the formation was named.

Some 40 million years before present, Idaho began to be pulled apart in an east-west direction. Giant blocks of the earth's crust dropped, forming intermontane valleys, while other parts were uplifted to create fault-block mountain ranges like the West Mountains, Lost River and Lemhi ranges. Beginning with this period, known as the Tertiary, the climate became extremely arid. Few streams flowed out of the region and sediments washed from the surrounding mountains began to fill up the valleys. Camels and horses roamed the arid grasslands that dominated much of southern Idaho. Their bones are readily found in the valley fill deposits common to the intermontane valleys of the region.

At the beginning of the Miocene epoch, approximately 25 million years ago, a giant rift zone opened up in eastern Oregon. Floods of basalt, a rock of volcanic origins, poured out over Oregon, Washington and the western edge of Idaho to form what geographers call the Columbia River Plateau. These basalts are seen in the lower Clearwater River valley, by the southeast end of Coeur d'Alene Lake and elsewhere. The age of the basalt and other volcanics becomes progressively younger from the west to east. In more recent times, basalt floods also covered southern Idaho to form the Snake River Plain. Some of these flows are less than 1,000 years old.

By the beginning of the Pleistocene Ice Age some 2.5 million years ago, most of the major geological features of Idaho were already in place. No new mountain ranges have been uplifted. No sea has inundated the land. Nevertheless, the Ice Age substantially changed the outward appearance of existing landscape features. In somewhat the way that new clothes can change the appearance of a person's

body without altering the structure beneath, glaciers transformed the basic landscape into an entirely new look. Mantles of snow were in—desert landforms were out.

Glaciers changed the face of many Idaho mountains. They scraped and sharpened the mountain peaks and valleys into horns, cirque basins, U-shaped valleys and aretes. Some of the best examples of glacial scouring and land forms can be seen in the Sawtooth Mountains, Big Horn Crags, Selway Crags, Lemhi, Bitterroot, Pioneer, White Cloud, Payette Crest and Beaverhead mountains. Only the higher elevations were glaciated; many lower mountain ranges were untouched and tend to be rounder, lacking the rugged scenery that results from glaciation.

Left: Unglaciated, V-shaped canyon cut by the Selway River in the Selway-Bitterroot Wilderness. Below: Basalt, or extruded lava, columns along the Boise River. GEORGE WUERTHNER PHOTOS

11

As a glacier slowly moves down a canyon from its source high in the mountains, it plucks rocks and boulders from the surrounding hillsides. This accumulated material, called a moraine, is deposited along the snout and margins of the glacier when it melts. Here a horseshoe-shaped terminal moraine can be seen as the low unforested hill at the mouth of a Lemhi Range canyon. GEORGE WUERTHNER

GLACIATION

Probably no other geomorphological process has had a more dramatic effect on Idaho's mountain scenery than glaciation. Unglaciated mountains tend to have roundish features, V-shaped water-carved canyons and few lakes. Glaciers, on the other hand, steepened head-walls of canyons, deepened stream canyons, sharpened peaks and created lakes.

Glaciers form when more snow remains each year than melts away. If given enough years, the snow will compact and turn to ice. When enough ice and snow is piled up, the glacial ice actually becomes somewhat plastic and begins to flow outward—like toothpaste squeezing from a tube. As these glaciers flow over bedrock and boulders, the bottom layer of ice constantly thaws and refreezes and some of the rocks and boulders are frozen into the ice and plucked from the mountainside. These rocks, boulders and gravel are carried downstream with the moving iceflow, as on a huge conveyor belt. In mountains, glaciers usually flow down existing stream beds, but steepen the walls and flatten the bottom to create a classic U-shaped valley. Eventually a point is reached where the ice melts as fast as it flows downward and an equilibrium is reached. Here the glacier deposits the rocks and gravels, called moraine, which it has removed from higher up the mountain.

Perhaps the easiest glacial features to recognize are cirques. These bowl-shaped amphitheaters look as if a giant ice cream scoop had taken away a chunk of the mountainside. Cirques are formed by the constant plucking action of the glacier, which eventually steepens the back of a basin, while rounding out the floor. Frequently, small moraine dams or bedrock walls will hold back water in the bottom of the basin to form a tiny tarn or cirque lake.

If two cirque glaciers are back to back with a

Contrary to popular opinion, the Ice Ages were not times of extreme cold, but rather of a cool and wet climate similar to that found today along the British Columbia coast. The heavy precipitation and constant cloud cover allowed winter snows to accumulate to great depth and eventually change to ice. During the height of the glacial period, ice sheets and cirque glaciers buried most of Idaho's higher peaks and, in some cases, the ice even overrode entire mountain ranges. One such lobe of ice, spreading south from Canada, covered most of northern Idaho and helped to scour out the basins now occupied by Lake Pend Oreille and other lakes of north Idaho.

The generally higher precipitation that accompanied the Ice Age, combined with the melting of the glaciers, increased the flows of Idaho's rivers. Many, like the Middle Fork of the Salmon and South Fork of the Clearwater, accelerated their down-cutting and created steep-sided canyons in dissected plateaus like those found in the Boise, Coeur d'Alene, Clearwater and Salmon River mountains.

12

Rock and gravel embedded in glacial ice scours and scratches bedrock surfaces, as here on granite in the Sawtooths. WILLIAM MULLINS

ridge separating them, the constant grinding and tearing away at their headwalls will produce a narrow razor-edge known as an arete. If three or more glaciers carve and pluck away at several sides of a mountain, a pyramid-shaped peak results, similar to the Matterhorn in Europe. These are called "horns" in reference to the famous Swiss mountain.

Embedded in the bottom of the moving glacier are rocks, gravel and boulders, all acting like sandpaper to smooth and polish the bedrock beneath the ice. Recently deglaciated bedrock will sometimes shine like a mirror as a result of this abrasion. By noting the general trend of these parallel scratches which John Muir called "the tracks of glaciers," one can determine the direction of ice flow.

Today in Idaho there are few active glaciers, small remnant patches of ice and permanent snowfields. But the effects of glaciation are widespread and have greatly enhanced the beauty of Idaho's mountains.

When two glaciers occupy opposite sides of a peak, their separate grinding may create a narrow, knife-edged ridge along the backs of the opposing cirque basins. The result, known as an arete, is seen here from Blodgett Peak in the Selway-Bitterroot Wilderness. GEORGE WUERTHNER

3

WEATHER

Heavy precipitation and cloudy skies dominate northern Idaho mountains. The narrow valleys, like those of the forested Coeur d'Alene Mountains (seen here near Lookout Pass), wring moisture from the air masses as they rise and cool in crossing. JEFF GNASS

Climate influences the kind of weathering mountains receive and, hence, affects the overall appearance of mountains. Geomorphic features such as glacial landforms or alluvial fans are only two examples of this effect. But mountains also influence the climate. Much of the variability in climatic conditions can be attributed to the changes mountains create on weather. In essence, mountains make their own weather and a look at a few representative mountain communities will show this.

For example, Challis, surrounded by mountains in the central part of the state, averages only 7.5 inches of precipitation a year, making it Idaho's driest reporting weather station. Wallace, the wettest station, located in the Coeur d'Alene Mountains of northern Idaho, receives some 46.1 inches of annual precipitation, which is still less than the annual precipitation (52 inches) of Memphis, Tennessee. Although precipitation usually increases with elevation because of orographic lift, elevation alone does not guarantee more moisture. Compare Challis, at 5,175', and Wallace at 2,770'. The more important factor is where the town is located relative to prevailing air masses and surrounding mountain ranges.

Wallace is at the upper end of the Coeur d'Alene River valley, which opens to the west—the direction from which moisture-bearing air masses arrive from the Pacific Ocean. The mountains behind Wallace are the first elevational barrier encountered by these air masses after crossing the Cascades. As they flow up the Coeur d'Alene valley and over the mountains, they rise, cool and drop their moisture as rain or snow on the west slope. Thus Wallace has more than adequate annual precipitation.

Unlike Wallace, Challis is located in a mountain bowl surrounded on all sides by high peaks. No matter which direction precip-

itation-bearing winds come from, they must rise over some mountain barrier, dropping most of their water content by the time they reach the Challis area. In addition, as air masses begin to descend a mountain barrier they expand and warm, increasing their ability to absorb moisture. Thus such winds actually suck up moisture and dry the downwind slope of a mountain even more. (Such warm, drying winds are a regular feature of the east slope of the Rockies from Alberta to Wyoming, and are called Chinooks or snow-eaters because of their ability to rapidly melt winter snowpacks.) As a result of this phenomenon, called the rain shadow

affect, the lee sides of mountain barriers are usually very dry. Anyone familiar with the west can think of places where the rain shadow effects are pronounced: California's Owens Valley just east of the cloud-ripping Sierras, the sunny east slope of the Cascades, the San Luis Valley just east of the lofty San Juan Mountains of Colorado; all are examples of regions lying in the rain shadow of high mountains. For comparison to Challis, Deadwood Dam (approximately 90 miles west and only 200' higher in elevation) lies closer to the west slope of the mountains. It receives 32.3 inches of annual precipitation—more than four

times the Challis total!

The Challis area is, in effect, a cold, dry, desert. Even Tucson, Arizona, is wetter—with an annual average of 10 to 12 inches of precipitation. Though most people visiting Challis for the first time might note its aridity, few would consider it a desert. The surrounding mountains may keep moisture from falling on Challis itself, but they also act as reservoirs storing water as snowfall. Throughout the long, cloudless summers, the hay fields and meadows surrounding Challis remain green because life-giving water flows out of the mountains as snowmelt. In addition, Challis's higher latitude (45 degrees N), halfway between the equator and the pole, means its evaporation rate is less than Tucson's. There may be less water falling upon Challis than on Tucson, but less goes further this far north.

Mountains affect precipitation in yet another way. Wallace is located in a narrow valley; Challis in a wide-open bowl. Narrow valleys, typical of northern Idaho, squeeze moisture out

Above: Sub-zero weather is rare near Dubois, where the Snake River Plain meets the Beaverheads.
Below: Stanley, in a high mountain basin, is among the coldest locations. GEORGE WUERTHNER PHOTOS

of air masses in much the same way as mountain barriers do. In addition, less evaporation occurs in the shady recesses of narrow valleys. Thus Coeur d'Alene, at approximately the same latitude as Wallace, but located 50 miles west in a more open valley location, receives only 26 inches of annual precipitation, almost half of Wallace's yearly average. The state's highest precipitation is thought to occur in the narrow canyons on the west slope of the Bitterroot Mountains, where an average of 90 inches or more occurs.

Idaho is strongly influenced by its proximity to the moderating effects of the Pacific Ocean maritime climate. Northern Idaho in particular has a relatively mild climate for its far northern location. Midwinter temperatures here average 20 to 25 degrees warmer than similar northern locations in North Dakota. And even northern Maine is 15 to 20 degrees colder, on the average, than northern Idaho. The mild, moist air masses from the Pacific sweep over northern Idaho for extended periods

16

in the winter, bringing cloudy, snowy weather with temperatures hovering around the freezing point. Northern Idaho is, in fact, one of the cloudiest places in the United States during the winter months, averaging only 30 percent sunshine and in some winters, as little as 10 percent sunshine. Even coastal Seattle sees more sun, with an average of 20 percent sunshine during its cloudiest month of December.

The maritime influence can be seen in Idaho's yearly temperature differences. Sandpoint in the north experiences an average of 65 degrees Fahrenheit in July and 26 degrees in January, a difference of 39 degrees. Challis, under a more continental climate regime, has a July average of 68 degrees and a January average of 20 degrees, for a yearly difference of 48 degrees. Yet few places in Idaho experience extremes like the northern Great Plains, where a community like Westby, Montana, sees a 68-degree variation between its July and January averages.

Southern Idaho experiences a still more continental climate. The southeast, farthest from the Pacific, is where the state's greatest extremes are found. Here, cold, relatively sunny winters and hot, rainless summers prevail. Island Park, located in a mountain valley near the infamously frigid West Yellowstone, Montana, has the Idaho record low of minus 60 degrees.

Cold, arctic air masses frequently flow down from Canada and settle in over much of southern and central Idaho during the winters. Occasionally these arctic fronts will also deflect northern Idaho's prevailing maritime air masses and push into this part of the state, bringing nighttime lows of 20 or more degrees below zero. It is during these arctic fronts when panhandle record lows of 35 below and 34 below were recorded for Sandpoint and Coeur d'Alene, respectively. The winter low I experienced when I lived along the Big Lost River near Mackay in the central part of the state was only a few degrees cooler, at 42 below.

As cold air settles into the valleys, temperature inversions, with their attendant air pollution hazards, are an unpleasant fact in

The mild maritime climate of northern Idaho results in dense, lush forests, home to western red cedar and thimbleberry. GEORGE WUERTHNER

many urban and rural areas of Idaho. The cold air drains into the mountain-rimmed valleys and becomes trapped by overriding warmer air masses. Skiers are well aware of the phenomenon. Driving from frigid, stagnate, smoky air of the cities, they gain elevation heading toward their favorite mountain, and usually drive out of the smog and onto warm, sunny slopes. The increased wood-stove use during recent years has contributed to an unprecedented winter air pollution problem in many Idaho cities. Ironically, air pollution then feeds itself, since the woodsmoke particulates act as nuclei for the formation of ice fog, which helps to trap even more pollution.

Summer temperatures throughout Idaho vary considerably with aspect and elevation. As a rule, the higher one goes in the mountains, the cooler the overall temperature. Thus Ashton, at 5,220' elevation, has a July average of 63.7 degrees, which compares with Boise's (elevation 2,838') July average of 74.5 degrees. Nighttime averages are considerably lower. Obsidian (elevation 6,870') in the Sawtooth Valley has an average July minimum of 36 degrees. Over all of Idaho during the summer the clear skies and dry air mean nighttime cooling is extreme, with diurnal differences of 30 to 40 degrees. This means an 80-degree day may cool to 40 degrees by early morning, making temperatures comfortable for sleeping, but marginal for growing gardens—especially in the higher mountain valleys.

The warmest temperatures in the state have been recorded in the Clearwater River valley, with Lewiston having a record of 117 and Orofino once hitting 118 degrees. This compares to a record high of "only" 110 for Los Angeles, California, a city much farther south, and it equals the Phoenix, Arizona, all-time high of 118. But many mountain valleys will at times experience relatively high temperatures. The record high for Hailey, just south of Sun Valley, is 109. Salmon has a record of 106, McCall 104. And even Ashton, located in the Henry's Fork valley of southeast Idaho, has a high reading of 100 degrees.

The general aridity of Idaho, particularly in the south, would pose a serious handicap to human settlement were it not for the snow-catching attributes of the state's mountains. The water from winter snowpacks provides the constant stream flow essential for life during the summer drought period, with nearly 98 percent of the water utilization going to irrigate Idaho crops and lawns. In addition, these mountain waters run the state's many hydro-electric dams and provide river recreation on such famous streams as the Snake, Middle Fork of the Salmon, Lochsa and Selway.

Overall, Idaho's mountain climate is much more pleasant than those of most of the midwest, southeast and New England states, and is undoubtedly one the state's best kept secrets.

4

VEGETATION

I remember asking an old cowboy I met by the Albion Range in southern Idaho about what plants I could expect to find in the nearby mountains. He replied, "Boy, all you need to know is that in northern Idaho they got trees and down here all we got is grass." This is a simplification, of course, but certainly an accurate generalization. Overall, southern Idaho's mountains are arid and thus dominated by grasses and shrubs, while the northern mountains are covered with a lush forest growth. And from a cowboy's perspective, one doesn't need to know much more, for the grassy mountains of the south support Idaho's livestock industry, while the forested peaks of the north are the domain of the logger. Yet within these broad divisions there are some distinct distributional patterns to note.

For example, the northern Idaho forests are very similar botanically to the West Coast temperate rainforest. Here grow western red cedar, mountain hemlock, western hemlock and grand fir typical of the forests in the Cascades. Growing in the understory are devil's club, thimbleberry, huckleberry and ferns. Along with these species we find the trees of the Inland Empire: western larch and western white pine and a species more typical of the boreal forests to the north—paper birch. Then there are ubiquitous species, trees you might find in Colorado or Oregon, Montana or Utah: ponderosa pine, lodgepole pine, Douglas fir, and subalpine fir. These trees are widely distributed not only in northern Idaho, but also the entire state. At the other extreme is a relatively rare tree, the timberline-dwelling subalpine larch, which is limited in distribution to a few high mountain ranges in Idaho, Montana, Washington and nearby Canadian ranges.

Contrasting to the dense tall timber of northern Idaho, southern Idaho's arid mountains are the domain of grasses and juniper,

Idaho is the most heavily forested of the western states and its forests support a widespread timber industry. Seen here are subalpine fir in the Sawtooth Mountains. JEFF GNASS

18

Because of the great elevational differences in Idaho, from less than 1,000' to more than 12,000', some type of wild floral display is in bloom from March until September as spring advances up the mountainsides. Pictured here are paintbrush, balsamroot and lomatium near Grangeville. GEORGE WUERTHNER

19

Ponderosa pine grows where fires once occurred at 10- to 15-year intervals. Thick bark and lack of low branches protect mature trees. GEORGE WUERTHNER

with sagebrush associates dominating a landscape reminiscent of Utah or Nevada. Yet, despite what the old cowboy said, one can find trees including aspen, Douglas fir, subalpine fir, whitebark pine, limber pine, lodgepole pine and Englemann spruce. But few southern Idaho mountain ranges will have the abundance and diversity of plant life that is typical of the north. For example, only Douglas fir, subalpine fir and juniper grow in the Owyhee Mountains of southwest Idaho, while a typical northern Idaho range might have all these species plus a dozen more.

Aspect, elevation and other factors also influence what tree or plant is found where. For example, south-facing slopes are both drier and warmer than north slopes, so it is not uncommon to find grasslands dominating them, sometimes to the top of a mountain, while the north slope is covered with forests. In addition, the higher one goes, the colder and windier it usually becomes and only plants adapted to these conditions survive. So, near timberline we find trees like the subalpine larch and whitebark pine growing. These trees grow slowly, have sturdy roots to cling to the windy peaks and adaptations for survival in the short growing season of these elevations.

Many site micro-climates alter these generalizations. For example, one might find western red cedar, a tree that prefers moist habitats, growing along the bottom of a narrow, shady canyon, with ponderosa pine, a tree of open, dry areas, growing on the slope a few hundred yards away. But if one were to measure temperatures, soil moisture and percentage of sunshine in each location, great differences would be seen. The cedar would occupy a basically wet site while the pine had an arid environment.

Trees are long-lived species and thus not necessarily good indicators of present microclimatic conditions. For example, many mature ponderosa pine in central Idaho got their start on dry, open sites after forest fires opened up the canopy. Today this same pine might be surrounded by a forest of younger Douglas fir

and grand fir, species that tolerate some shade and require higher moisture levels than the pine. This progressive change in the dominance of plant species is called succession. The sequence is somewhat predictable, but is modified by many factors, including the availability of seed sources.

For example, after a fire in the aspen-fir forests of southeast Idaho, we can expect a predictable progression. First, aspen, a species that needs lots of sunshine for vigorous growth, will sprout on the burned-over site. Aspen grow fast, but lose their vigor as they mature and become susceptible to disease, usually within 100 years. If a fire fails to rejuvenate a stand, the overhead canopy closes, shading the forest floor, and makes the site unsuitable for the growth and survival of young aspen. In the understory of a closed canopy aspen grove, subalpine fir, which prefers wet, cool sites and grows well in the shade, will thrive and eventually replace aspen. The fir can continue to grow in its own shade and thus can perpetuate the fir forest until some natural or man-made factor destroys it.

If you have ever walked up a high mountain, you have, no doubt, noted a slow, gradual change in the kinds of vegetation that dominate each particular elevation. These transformations correspond to a change in moisture, soils and temperature that is roughly equivalent to traveling 300 miles farther north for every 1,000 feet of elevation gained. Thus a hike from the grasslands in the Lost River valley, at 6,000', to the windswept treeless summit of Mt. Borah at more than 12,600' would be analogous to getting into a car and driving 1,800 miles north. From Idaho, such a drive would place you squarely on the Arctic Ocean, so it's no surprise that at high elevations in the state's mountains, one sees alpine plants like moss campion and mountain avens, the same species that grow at sea level along the northern coast of Canada.

A hypothetical hike from the bottom of Hells Canyon on the Snake River, at 2,000', to the top of He Devil Mountain, at better than

Left: Black cottonwood, common along Idaho's waterways, provides shade, streambank stability and homes for wildlife, and readily sprouts anew from cuttings. JEFF GNASS
Above: The weathered trunk of a dead limber pine near timberline on Mt. Borah is probably hundreds of years old. The cold, arid environment makes decomposition exceedingly slow and limits nutrients available for soil in alpine areas.
GEORGE WUERTHNER

9,000', would allow you to pass through nearly every major biome represented in Idaho's mountains. Along the Snake are grasslands dominated by bluebunch wheatgrass and Idaho fescue. Gain some elevation, say to 4,000', and you enter the ponderosa pine zone dominated by open, park-like stands of old pine interspersed with grasses. Keep climbing higher and the next tree species you will encounter is Douglas fir, with some grand fir intermixed on wetter sites. Now we are up to 6,000' and tree cover is more or less continuous. At around 7,000' you notice that the meadows are lush and full of flowers and the trees are narrow-spiked so as to shed the deep snows that fall at these heights. The tree with the narrow spike-like crown is subalpine fir.

If you're like me, by the time you reach 8,500', you will probably be breathing hard—at this altitude most people begin to feel the effects of thin air. Up here, the growing season is extremely short, few trees survive, and the ones that do are stunted and shorter than their cousins a thousand feet lower. Besides the fir, you notice another tree, the whitebark pine. It has an open and airy appearance, with sturdy roots and short, thick trunks, and seems to prefer windswept ridges at the limits of tree growth. It's not much farther to the top and the trees are really noticeably sparse. Near the summit, where the winds blow most of the year, you find a bit of alpine tundra: low matted flowers and shrubs clinging to nooks and crannies, trying to survive where no tree can manage a living. If you make this entire hike, you will have passed through plant communities and climates similar to the desert grasslands of Utah, the boreal forests of Canada and the tundra of the arctic. It's quite a journey and it probably did not take you longer than a day.

Although Idaho's mountains have a rich and varied flora, there has been a substantial change from its former composition and structure. Three human influences have altered the land: logging, grazing and fire suppression.

Logging has altered age structure and species

Above: Blossoms of serviceberry, whose branches are browsed by elk and deer.
Below: On public lands in the Boulder Mountains, this bare muddy area probably once was filled with willows. GEORGE WUERTHNER PHOTOS

composition of the forestlands. For the most part, except in designated wilderness where logging is not permitted, old growth trees (more than 250 years old) are becoming scarce. In addition, certain species are favored in reforestation programs, with a resulting change in the proportions of various species.

In reading the journals of early explorers and travelers who ventured across the mountain areas of what is now southern Idaho, one is struck by how often these people noted lush grasslands in areas that today are dominated by sagebrush and other shrubs. The change from grasslands to shrublands can be, in many places, attributed to the introduction of domestic livestock and the subsequent overgrazing. It would be wrong to imply that sagebrush did not occur in the mountains of Idaho prior to the advent of livestock, but when too many animals are on the range, grasses are eaten, while sagebrush is ignored, eventually giving the competitive advantage to the shrub.

The changing of grasslands into deserts is occurring more rapidly in the United States than in the much-publicized north of Africa, but such changes are slow and incremental, unlike the major alteration in plant structure that accompanies logging. A hillside devoid of trees is highly visible, but the changes that accompany years of overgrazing are harder to see. Native grass species like bluebunch wheatgrass may be replaced with non-native, less desirable species like cheatgrass. Grasses may even disappear entirely, to be replaced by sagebrush and juniper. Riparian vegetation, like willows, often suffers because of tramping and browsing. Without willows to bind them together, streambanks erode, which results in wider, shallower creeks. The water table may drop, resulting in the further elimination of water-dependent species. Many of these changes would not be noticed even in an entire human lifetime, but they are nevertheless taking place and the overall productivity of the land is suffering.

The mountains of Idaho were severely overgrazed in the late 1800s and early 1900s

Right: Double timberline in the Lost River Range, where lower elevations are too dry and upper ones too cold for trees.
Below: The autumn colors of an aspen grove in the White Cloud Mountains.
GEORGE WUERTHNER PHOTOS

and some have never recovered. This decline in rangeland health was partly from greed and partly from ignorance. The early ranchers were optimistic and tended to treat the western ranges like eastern pasturelands. Eastern pastures recovered rapidly from heavy grazing because of greater rainfall and better soils. In 1884, J. Elliot, writing about the Owyhee Mountains of southwest Idaho, noted: "The ranchers collected about them some stock, and while they slept their stock increased rapidly. Cattlemen hearing of the excellent ranges for stock, drove cattle in here in large numbers. The summer range for cattle is almost inexhaustible, every hillside furnishing a luxuriant growth of bunch grass."

Of course those who are familiar with the Owyhee Mountains today would be hard-pressed to recall where they have ever seen hillsides covered with "a luxuriant growth of bunch grass," and the same is all too frequently true for many other of the arid southern Idaho mountains. Of course not all of Idaho's mountain grasslands are suffering from overgrazing, and some of them are in excellent condition, but these are the exception rather than the rule.

It's worthwhile to track down plots of ungrazed ranges where fencelines provide clear boundaries between grazed and ungrazed grassland communities. The best places to find these remnants of Idaho's mountain grasslands is to locate old cemeteries, railroad rights-of-way and special exclosures such as exist in the upper West Fork of Mink Creek in the Bannock Range by Pocatello and along Pole Creek in the upper Sawtooth Valley. Where livestock have been fenced out, one usually notices a much higher percentage of grass cover and little, if any, sagebrush. In addition, creeks flowing through such exclosures will frequently be deep-

23

ALPINE LARCH

A tree most people will never see is the alpine larch, although its close relative the western larch is a common species in the lower-elevation forests from McCall northward. Unlike its widely distributed cousin, the alpine larch has strict habitat requirements, thriving on rocky, north-facing slopes above 6,000'. Since many of the northern Idaho mountain ranges rise barely above this elevation, the alpine larch distribution is restricted at best. They are found in few ranges other than the Bitterroot, Selkirk and Cabinet. Although many of the mountains south of the Salmon River are high enough, they are apparently too dry to meet the species' habitat needs.

The most distinctive feature of both larches is their deciduous habit. In the fall, their short needles turn gold and drop off, leaving the branches bare all winter. For the alpine larch this means the growing season is short—a scant 90 days over most of its range—and as a result the tree is extremely slow growing. One larch studied was only six feet tall, yet 280 years old! Another tree, which measured seven inches in diameter, was 586 years old; the oldest individuals may survive a thousand years.

This longevity is necessary since alpine larch do not produce their first seed until they are nearly 100 years old (as compared to a lodgepole pine, which can produce viable seeds within five to 10 years) and germination success is extremely poor. In one experiment only two seedlings were produced from 5,000 seeds planted. Successful germination and establishment of seedlings occurs irregularly and at widely spaced intervals—perhaps every few decades.

Should a seedling manage to establish itself on a rocky substrate typical of its habitat, it will invest most of its energy in developing a deep and extensive root system to survive the

GEORGE WUERTHNER

summer droughts common to northern Idaho mountains. In addition, by remaining short the young larch benefits from deep winter snows and avoids the desiccating and abrasive winds common at these elevations. Once the roots are firmly entrenched, the tree begins to grow taller.

Although producing new needles each spring is energy-expensive, deciduous needles are more efficient in photosynthesis than evergreen needles. In the short growing season of timberline, any increase in photosynthetic capacity is an ecological advantage. Winter needle loss also

allows the bare branches to shed snow easily—a distinct plus in the heavy snow belt within the tree's natural range. No needles also means no water loss in winter when replacement from the frequently frozen soil is impossible. Finally, the bare branches act as a sieve instead of a sail, allowing the gale-force winds common at timberline to pass through the tree unobstructed.

All of these adaptations have allowed the alpine larch to colonize habitat few other trees can tolerate, carving out an uncontested niche for itself.

er and narrower, with banks lined by thick riparian vegetation such as willow, while those outside of the exclusion will often be wider and shallower—less suitable for trout and other game fish.

The third major human influence upon Idaho's vegetation has been the suppression of wild fires. Prior to the advent of modern firefighting activities, thousands of acres of Idaho's forests and rangelands burned annually. Many mountain plant communities are adapted to periodic fires and some even depend upon them. Rather than laying the land to waste, fires served many beneficial purposes including recycling nutrients, thinning trees, cleansing forest pathogens and creating natural fire breaks where fuel loading was reduced.

Unlike in the humid east, where almost everything organic rots whether you want it to or not, Idaho's hot, dry summer hinders decomposition of plant litter. Dead leaves, branches, grasses and needles build up faster than micro-organisms can break them down, and the nutrients tied up in slowly decaying material are unavailable for plant growth. Fires served as the main nutrient cycling agent in the arid west prior to the intervention of the European. Without fire, many plant communities are nutrient poor.

An occasional fire was a hot, all-consuming blaze, particularly at higher elevations where fires are less frequent. But more commonly, the fires were small, quick-burning affairs that seldom killed the larger trees. These fires eliminated the dead litter on the forest floor, killed some of the smaller trees and only scarred the old forest giants. Today scientists count the fire scars on these old forest veterans as a means of determining the relative frequency of past fires. The trees that survived these burns grew faster and were healthier since they had fewer rivals for light, water and nutrients. Old photographs show that many of Idaho's low-elevation ponderosa pine and Douglas fir forests consisted of large, mature trees growing in open, park-like stands—in contrast to the dense, thick, spindly forests

that characterize these same areas today.

Prior to fire suppression, wild fires were ignited by lightning as well as by Indians. In fact, at low elevations, humans may have been the dominant cause of fires. Indians ignited fires to clear away brush and deadfall, to stimulate the growth of grasses for horsefeed and to attract grazing wildlife like bison close to established villages, and in warfare to distract enemies or prevent them from giving chase. Research of low-elevation ponderosa pine forests shows an average of one fire every five to 10 years. Even the forests at higher, moister elevations burned at 30- to 40-year intervals.

Many of the early Idaho explorers mention the frequency of wild fire. For example Osborn Russell, a trapper, writing in his journal about the Pocatello area in September of 1834, notes: "the country very smoky and the weather sultry and hot." In the same year, naturalist John Townsend passed through the Big Wood River valley south of Hailey and wrote: "... on the main prairie scarcely a blade of grass could be found, it having lately been fired by the Indians to improve the crops [grass] of next year."

The frequent fires not only recycled nutrients and reduced the incidence of large catastrophic fires, but also helped to cleanse the forest. Some forest pathogens are killed just by smoke! Others, such as burrowing insects, are killed by the heat. The current epidemics of lodgepole beetle infestations are partially the result of fire suppression, which has promoted the fire-free environment ideal for the development of these insects. In essence, fire keeps the forest thinned and healthy and performs the same function as the wolf, which helps to keep deer herds healthy and within the carrying capacity of their ranges.

Fires also frequently burned through rangelands and many grasses are particularly adapted to reseeding a slope after a fire. Fire suppression, combined with overgrazing, which eliminated fuels, has eliminated fire from many areas. One result has been the expansion of juniper and sagebrush, both fire-intolerant

species, onto many former grassland sites. Frequently these juniper and sage invasion areas are considered undesirable as grazing sites and management agencies spend thousands of dollars yearly to chain, spray or otherwise control these species, while they also expend energy and money fighting fires that created the situation in the first place.

In the future one can expect these attitudes to change as the notion that fires may be good gradually is accepted. Already, in many of Idaho's wilderness areas, natural fires are frequently allowed to burn uncontrolled, although monitored, and a great deal of positive information has been gleaned from these studies.

As we learn more about the natural role of wild fires and the direct benefits associated with an unlogged forest, a lightly grazed grassland and the importance of maintaining a healthy ecosystem, many of Idaho's mountain vegetative communities will undoubtedly recover much of their former quality and vigor and perhaps once again people will be able to visit places like the Owyhee Mountains and write about the "luxuriant growth of bunch grasses" covering the slopes.

JAMES K. MORGAN

FIRE ECOLOGY

Prior to the advent of modern fire suppression, wild fires were a common and pervasive ecological force in the west. Thousands of acres burned in an average summer and every 30 to 40 years a "fire summer" would occur, when weather conditions led to millions of acres' burning. Forest and range ecological communities were adapted to these periodic fires and many depended upon them for long-term survival. No single human influence (except perhaps overgrazing) has destroyed the natural intregrity of the Rocky Mountain ecosystems more than fire suppression.

Old photos of Idaho's mountains show that most low-elevation forests of ponderosa pine and Douglas fir were open, park-like stands, with large, mature trees. The understory usually consisted of grasses. Studies of fire scars on old trees show that these habitats usually burned at five- to ten-year intervals, killing most of the saplings that had sprouted since the last fire, leaving the remaining trees in balance with the available water, soil nutrients and light.

Higher-elevation forests burned at less frequent intervals of 30 to 50 years. Because of higher fuel accumulations resulting from a longer burn interval, fires here were more catastrophic and, often, entire stands would be replaced. In many areas these higher-elevation stands were dominated by lodgepole pine, a rapidly growing species that matures early and can reseed an area quickly after a burn. The present widespread occurrence of pine beetle epidemics is partly the result of human interference with this process. Pine beetles usually attack mature lodgepole pine that live under crowded conditions. Prior to active fire suppression fires thinned or even replaced entire lodgepole stands before they reached maturity and susceptability to pine beetle infestation.

Fire rotations of less than a hundred years are the norm for most western forests, but very moist forest habitats such as old-growth western red cedar groves may not burn for hundreds or even a thousand years. Even these trees, however, may depend upon frequent fires for their long-term survival. In the past, frequent burns in drier forest habitats kept the accumulation of fuel low and fires swept through these forests quickly. Because of a lack of fuel, these fires seldom burned hot enough to invade moister, old-growth stands, hence many of the magnificent cathedral-like groves of western red cedar found in northern Idaho may exist because fires occurred regularly in adjacent forest types.

In most of Idaho, like much of the west, summer drought is common and the arid environment precludes rapid decomposition of dead litter. In the absence of biological breakdown of organic matter, nutrients remain locked up and unavailable for new plant growth. If the condition persists lo ng enough, growing trees and other plants begin to starve for essential nutrients. Growth slows. Reproduction stops. Diseases and other pathogens increasingly weaken or kill individuals. In the arid west there is usually only a short period of the year during the spring months when soils are moist and warm enough to provide decomposing organisms the proper environment for composting dead material. In the absence of bacteria, fungi and other decomposing agen ts, fires provide the mechanism for the breakdown of dead litter. At higher elevations, the cool, acid environment also suppresses biological breakdown of plant litter, hence even here fire is an impor tant nutrient-cycling agent.

Besides locking up nutrients, fire suppression actually increases the likelihood of a holocaust at some later date since fuel continues to build up and, when it is finally ignited, the blaze is hotter and even more difficult to control. Frequent burns also create natural firebreaks.

Many forest plants are adapted to fire. Ponderosa pine, Douglas fir and western larch try to survive fires. They have thick scaly or corky bark that protects the living inner layer of the tree. The larger, more mature trees are often limbless for a height of 30' or 40', so that low, slow fires are unlikely to ignite upper branches. Both adaptations protect these species from quick, low-fuel fires which were common prior to fire suppression.

Other plants are adapted to dominate a burned-over area by vigorous regeneration immediately after the burn cools. Aspen, for example, will sprout vigorously from its roots if a fire burns the crown. The ability to regenerate quickly after a fire was one advantage that grasses had over non-sprouting species of big sagebrush. Since natural ignition of grasslands usually occurred in late summer after the plants had dropped their seeds and gone dormant, fires did little actual damage. Living roots were protected below ground by the insulating soil. Usually in the spring after a burn, grasses would sprout new shoots.

With fire suppression, grasses no longer have the advantage, and sagebrush has increased in many areas accordingly. Because grasses are so flammable—in fact, almost depend upon fire for their ecological health—it was common government policy during the early years of the Forest Service to encourage overgrazing as a means of controlling fires. Overgrazed ranges did not burn well and so fires were indirectly suppressed. Many mountain meadows depend upon fire to clear away invading trees periodically, and with a reduction in burns, such forest clearings are disappearing.

Fires also stimulate the growth of many wildlife food sources. For example, elk and deer are primarily dependent upon brush and browse that invade burned-over areas. For 20 or 30 years after a fire the elk or deer herds will often increase because of improved nutrition. This is exactly what happened in northern

Sawtooth wilderness. Grasses in areas with naturally occurring fire cycles have a chance to establish, whereas fire suppression reduces grasses' natural advantage to establish in burned-over areas. Notice the height of the branches of these lodgepole pines, probably trained upwards by natural non-devastating grass fires. JEFF GNASS

growth. The increased incidence of spruce budworm epidemics, pine beetle epidemics and other forest pathogens can be attributed, in part, to the changing ecological conditions and generally weakened condition of today's forestland. As a wolf thins and maintains a healthy deer herd, fire thins and maintains a healthy forest.

There is not only an ecological cost to fire fighting, but also a genuine financial cost. The 65,000-acre Mortar Creek Fire along the Salmon River in 1979 cost $5.5 million to suppress! Yet most fire research has shown that suppression activities have nothing to do with controlling a blaze. Large fires stop because the weather changes, or they encounter a previously burned area and run out of fuel—seldom because of human interference. Some 95 percent of all fires burn fewer than 100 acres before going out of their own accord.

There are other costs associated with fire suppression. Many of the deficit timber sales occurring in Idaho are aimed at controlling pine beetle epidemics. The trees harvested are usually not commercially attractive and without government subsidies few of these timber sales would find buyers. Fire suppression created the environmental conditions favorable to pine beetle infestation; with further fire control, the condition will only persist, requiring continued deficit timber harvest. In addition, many of these timber sales are within presently roadless areas under consideration for wilderness designation, so that besides the actual logging costs, there is a hidden cost in the loss of wild country.

A more enlightened attitude towards fire is developing. Indeed, it may not be long before we begin to read news stories that tell about how a forest fire today "rejuvenated 100 acres" instead of "damaged 100 acres." In essence, Smokey the Bear lied. Rather than damaging the environment, fires create wildlife habitat and maintain healthy forests.

Idaho after the 1910 Burn. Elk herds prospered with the creation of large shrub communities, but declined as forest cover began to replace the brush 40 to 50 years after the original fires. Even grizzlies depend upon fire-induced food species: huckleberries, an important grizzly food in many areas of northern Idaho, readily invade areas after burns.

Many of the "managed" forests of today are actually quite unhealthy. The lack of fires has contributed to overstocked stands that lack sufficient light, water, and soil for maximum

5

WILDLIFE

A friend of mine just returned from a trip to New Zealand. The scenery was magnificent, she said, but she missed the wildlife. My friend never heard the chatter of squirrels in the forest, or the shuffle of a mouse in the leaves at night. There were no animals to fear or marvel at like the grizzly. An island far from any continental land mass, New Zealand has no native animals, except a limited diversity of birds. It has plenty of mountains, but as my friend learned, mountains without wildlife are just dead scenery.

Fortunately Idaho's mountains are more than just postcard material, and are alive with a tremendous array of wildlife including over 100 mammals and more than 300 bird species. In the dense, lush forests of the north one finds caribou and boreal owls, while the arid southern mountains are inhabited by the kangeroo rat and scrub jay. When compared to the fauna of other states, Idaho is lucky indeed, for few species have been totally extirpated, and several, like the mule and whitetail deer, may actually be more abundant now than in the past. Nevertheless, the state's wildlife populations overall have gone through some disastrous declines since the arrival of the European and only a limited number of species have really recovered some of their former abundance.

In 1834 the trapper Osborn Russell passed through the Pocatello area and recorded seeing "thousands of buffaloe." Nathaniel Wyeth, Captain Bonneville, Jedediah Smith, and other travelers who left behind records all mention an abundance of antelope, bison, grizzly bear, and bighorn sheep encountered during their travels in Idaho.

Mountain lions, found throughout Idaho, have been known to travel 300 miles seeking vacant territory to claim for their own hunting space. TIM CHRISTIE

Above: mule deer. GEORGE WUERTHNER
Right: Bull moose. ED WOLFF

Yet, fewer than a hundred years later—because of unrestricted hunting, trapping and habitat alterations, bison were extinct in the state, and other big game such as antelope, deer and elk were extremely rare. A news item in 1921 from southeast Idaho's *Caribou Notes* says: "The last Idaho legislature opened the deer season [after it was closed for years because of the virtual extinction of deer] in Bear Lake County for 1921-1922. Only about 3 bunches of deer are known to run in the county; one bunch of 8 or 9 head having made their headquarters in the mountains for the past several years only about 5 miles from the town of Montpelier." Today in this same general area, as all over Idaho, thousands of deer roam where fewer than 80 years ago a person could, quite literally, count the entire deer population of a mountain range on his two hands.

Deer were not the only big game species to suffer early declines because of hunting. Elk were nearly exterminated from the state and some authorities believe the statewide turn-of-the-century population was fewer than a thousand animals. Estimates from 1921 put elk numbers on the Clearwater National Forest at 200; on the St. Joe, 60; and on the Coeur d'Alene Forest, none. Elk transplants beginning in 1925

Top: Pronghorns, found in southern and south-central Idaho, can run 40 mph for brief bursts. JESS LEE
Below: Their horns consist of a bony core sheathed in material similar to human fingernails.
DARRELL GULIN

helped to spur a recovery and by the 1950s some 40,000 elk were thought to live on the Clearwater Forest alone. But since then elk population on the Clearwater has slipped to 15,000 animals for two main reasons: forage quality declined as forests invaded the shrublands early 20th century fires had created, and roading for timber harvest allowed huge increases in hunting pressure. Even with these declines there are far more elk in Idaho now than in the early 1900s. Elk are found in nearly all major mountain ranges except for those in southwest and southern Idaho.

Although deer and elk populations have increased from turn-of-the-century lows, another large herbivore—the bison—probably is gone forever as a wild component of Idaho's fauna. Early trappers reported herds numbering in the thousands in all the large intermontane valleys and the mountains near present-day Hailey, Challis and Salmon, down through the area of Pocatello, Bear Lake and Star Valley, near the Black Pine Range and elsewhere in eastern Idaho. Despite this abundance, the bison was essentially extinct in Idaho by the 1840s. Some authorities speculate the decline may have resulted from overkill by Indians who became more effective hunters once they acquired the horse.

Most people know about the disappearance of the bison, but few know that some 45 million antelope roamed North America—making the antelope nearly as numerous as the bison. Nevertheless antelope numbers reached a low of 13,000 by the 1920s. As in the rest of the west, Idaho's antelope have recovered and now number in the thousands. The largest herds are near the Lemhi and Lost River ranges, but smaller groups are scattered throughout the southern part of the state, particularly in the Owyhee country. While antelope are not usually considered mountain dwellers (they avoid forested, rocky terrain), they frequently wander

Left: A mature bull elk whose antlers are covered by a soft growth material called velvet. HARRY JARVIS
Below: Bighorn ram, who will battle only rams with horns of similar size and strength. TOM ULRICH

up to 9,000' or higher on open, sage-covered slopes.

Unlike antelope, which only occasionally enter the high country, moose are almost entirely restricted to Idaho's mountainous terrain. They are relatively common throughout the east-central, southeastern and northern parts of the state, but absent from the mountains of west-central and southwest Idaho. At the time of the mountain men, moose were either very scarce or non-existent in Idaho, for I could find no mention of them at all in any of the journals of these early explorers. It was not until 1908 when the biologist George Shiras described moose in Yellowstone that their presence in the Northern Rockies was verified.

From Yellowstone, moose apparently expanded their range and colonized much of the southeastern portion of the state, while other population centers in southern Canada contributed to the spread of moose into northern and central Idaho. Their long legs allow moose to travel in deeper snow than deer or elk; I have seen them wintering quite high (9,000') where they eat primarily browse: willow, aspen, and on occasion conifers like Douglas fir.

At first sight, the woodland caribou may be mistaken for moose. These animals are much rarer, however: only 30 are thought to roam the dense forests of northern Idaho's Selkirk Mountains. They are surprisingly tame and this quality may have contributed to their decimation by hunters, for caribou were once widely distributed throughout northern and central Idaho as far south as Elk City. Today hunting caribou is illegal, but the animals are threatened by the logging of old-growth timber, upon which grow lichens, their primary winter food.

Another mountain dweller, bighorn sheep, once had greater distribution and numbers. In some areas such as the Salmon River country of central Idaho early hunters reported bighorns to be more numerous than deer or elk. Bighorns were particularly hard-hit by the introduction of domestic cattle and sheep, which overgrazed their ranges. The bighorns succumbed easily to starvation, harsh weather and diseases carried by domestic stock.

Sheep are primarily grazers. Although they do eat an assortment of forage, they tend to be found where grasses are abundant—primarily in

Grizzly bear. JESS LEE   *Black bear.* ALAN CAREY

BEARS

In the days before the trappers and ranchers, grizzly bears were numerous throughout much of Idaho. They ranged through all the mountains of north, central, and southeast Idaho and even through such southerly areas as the Albion Range and the surrounding Snake River Plain. Bear Lake in southeast Idaho and Bear Valley near Stanley were both named for the abundance of grizzlies that once roamed these regions. Grizzlies used to gather in large groups along many Idaho rivers, including the Salmon, Lochsa, Clearwater and Boise, to feed upon the annual salmon runs. Today such congregations of bears can be observed only in Alaska. Osborn Russell noted in his journal that grizzlies appeared more numerous than black bears in the mountain regions he traveled back in the early 1800s.

Despite their early abundance, grizzlies were shot, poisoned and trapped to virtual extinction within the state. Today there are only a few parts of Idaho that have any grizzlies at all, and most of these are dispersers from British Columbia, Montana and Wyoming. Known or suspected grizzly bear populations occur in the extreme northern part of Idaho near the Canadian border, perhaps in the Bitterroot Mountains along the Montana-Idaho border and around Yellowstone National Park in the Island Park region.

While protection of habitat is essential to grizzly survival, this alone is not sufficient. In the large Selway-Bitterroot Wilderness, grizzlies were extirpated by the 1940s. Human-induced mortality is the single greatest threat to grizzlies and, even in sanctuaries like Yellowstone National Park, human-caused deaths are probably higher than bear populations can sustain.

Grizzlies tend to forage in open areas: avalanche paths, subalpine meadows and river bars. They are primarily vegetarian, although quite fond of meat if available and, in the spring, carrion is a choice food. The rest of the year they sustain themselves on berries, roots, pine nuts and insects. Carbohydrate levels are high in their diet and protein levels are low. Protein is essential for successful population growth and in the past the abundant salmon runs in Idaho's rivers provided this important nutritional element. With the loss of salmon runs, coupled with changes in vegetation patterns and the loss of many lower-elevation areas to human use, many of the surviving grizzly populations actually may be close to a negative nutritional balance. Hence, their reproductive rate and the survival of cubs is often marginal.

The black bear has fared better since the arrival of the European, perhaps partly because it prefers denser forests than the grizzly, which means the black bear is less likely to be seen and shot and also less likely to conflict with livestock. Black bears are found in all major mountain ranges, but are more numerous in northern Idaho.

inhabit high, rugged, remote mountain areas, they have not been subjected to the overhunting that other big-game species have suffered. In recent years, however, the spread of logging roads into subalpine basins has allowed hunters to invade the high country and some goat herds have declined dramatically.

Strict hunting regulations, transplanting, and amelioration of livestock competition allowed deer, elk, antelope and bighorns to regain some of their former abundance; many other species were not so fortunate. The wolf once was numerous and in Idaho its demise can be attributed partially to huge declines in game populations around the turn of the century, results of livestock introduction and over-hunting. As the wolf's natural prey disappeared it turned to hunting domestic animals. Stockmen gave little thought to their own culpability as they sought to resolve wolf-stock problems with poison, traps and guns. By the 1930s the wolf was no longer a breeding member of the Idaho fauna. Reports of single wolves and, occasionally, pairs continue but these animals are thought to be dispersing young males, not mated couples.

A Wolf Recovery Team, organized for the northern Rockies in 1973, has recently proposed wolf re-introductions for three areas: the Glacier Park-Bob Marshall Wilderness complex, Yellowstone National Park, and the central Idaho wilderness region. Each area is largely unroaded with very high game populations that could support several wolf packs. Biologically, they have great potential for wolf recovery. Politically, wolf re-introduction poses many obstacles, including almost universal resistance from livestock growers.

In recent years verified sightings, even photographs, attest to the presence of wolves on the Boise, Targhee, Challis and Clearwater national forests. And it is possible that a breeding population may actually re-establish itself in northern and central Idaho. But this is likely to occur only if breeding packs first re-colonize nearby northern Montana, from which both male and female wolves may disperse.

central and southern Idaho. The center of bighorn distribution is along the headwaters and tributaries of the Salmon River in the Salmon River Mountains, Lost River Range, and Boulder-White Cloud country. Sheep recently have been re-introduced into the canyons of Owyhee County in southwest Idaho and are expanding their range.

The mountain goat often seems to be confused with the bighorn, despite their strikingly different appearances. The white-furred goat has small, pointed, black horns while the tawny sheep carries sweeping, amber-colored horns. The goat is better adapted to cliff areas where winters bring deep, heavy snow, hence its greater abundance in northern Idaho. The bighorn prefers the more arid southern ranges. The natural range of the mountain goat did not extend any farther south than the high country near Ketchum, Mackay and Salmon; goats found in other parts of Idaho, such as the Snake River Range, are transplants. Because goats usually

Left: The rare lynx inhabits Idaho's densely forested areas, its population fluctuating with that of its prey, the snowshoe hare. ALAN CAREY
Above: Occasional wolves, usually roaming young males native to Canada, appear in the Clearwater and Salmon drainages. GEORGE WUERTHNER

Above: Yellow-bellied marmots are found throughout Idaho.
TIM CHRISTIE
Near right: Pikas will peer curiously at hikers, but are ready to hide.
GEORGE WUERTHNER
Far right:The wide-roaming wolverine is very rare in the state.
JESS LEE

34

Although wolves were trapped, poisoned and shot almost to extinction, other large predators were better able to cope with the invasion of humans. In Idaho's mountains one can still find black bears, mountain lions, coyotes, as well as lynxes, bobcats and grizzlies, although the latter three are rare.

Nearly all members of the weasel family are predators, but they were trapped primarily for their furs, not as varments. Heavy trapping combined with habitat deterioration nearly exterminated a number of species including the wolverine, otter, mink and marten, and the fisher was completely eliminated from the state. Today, thanks to more restrictive trapping regulations, as well as re-introductions, these species again can be found in Idaho, although not in great numbers. Both the wolverine and fisher are on the state sensitive species list, which means their numbers and distribution are limited.

Idaho's mountains are home to a host of rodents including the beaver, various ground squirrels, tree squirrels, voles, mice, bats, shrews and chipmunks. Four rabbit and hare species are commonly found in some mountains of the state: snowshoe hare, whitetailed jackrabbit, pygmy cottontail and Nuttall's cottontail.

In higher mountains one may encounter the pika, yellow-bellied marmot and hoary marmot. All three display a preference for rock slides and open areas, and thus are common above timberline. Pikas are small rabbit-like animals that feed on grasses and herbage. These tiny animals are active all winter and I have seen them basking in the sun in mid-February. When alarmed they emit a loud squeak and frequently scurry to the protection of the nearest rock pile. Pikas gather vegetation all summer, cure it under rocks and store for winter—thus their nickname of "haymaker."

Unlike pikas, marmots do hibernate. These groundhog-like creatures feed all summer, storing fat for the winter. Most marmots live in colonies composed of one large, dominant male, and several females with their young. When danger is sighted, a loud alarm whistle is sounded and all the animals within hearing dive into the nearest burrow for cover. The hoary marmot is found only at or above timberline in a few central and northern Idaho ranges, including the Bitterroot and Beaverhead, while the yellow-bellied is found at all elevations and in most ranges throughout the state, even on the Snake River Plain.

While the bird species of Idaho's mountains are too numerous to review, several rare or unusual species are worth mentioning. These include the whooping crane, which is occasionally seen around Gray's Lake; the trumpeter swan, found on the Henry's Fork; the great gray owl, which reaches its southern limits in the Big Hole Mountains; and the boreal owl, which has been found in the Salmon River Mountains.

Birds usually associated with dense forested mountains include the pileated woodpecker, winter wren, varied thrush, hermit thrush, golden-crowned kinglet, red-breasted nuthatch, mountain chickadee, Lewis' woodpecker, Steller's jay, red crossbill, pine grosbeak, spruce grouse, ruffed grouse, goshawk, western tanager, yellow-rumped warbler, Townsend's warbler and rufous hummingbird. In more arid grass- and sage-covered mountains are the sage grouse, red-tailed hawk, golden eagle, kestrel, mourning dove, common nighthawk, Say's phoebe, scrub jay, western bluebird, brown-headed cowbird, western meadowlark, horned lark, green-tailed towhee, sage sparrow, burrowing owl, Brewer's sparrow, vesper sparrow, raven, black-billed magpie, and short-earred owl.

Idaho's mountain streams and lakes are internationally famous for their fisheries. Trout fishing on the Henry's Fork near Island Park and on Silver Creek near Sun Valley draws fishermen from around the world. At one time nearly all of Idaho's rivers had salmon and steelhead runs, but dams, commercial overfishing, uncontrolled Indian treaty-rights fishing, sedimentation from logged-over headwaters and overgrazing of riparian habitats have nearly eliminated all wild runs. In recent

Top: Sandhill cranes mix with rare whooping cranes. JESS LEE *Left: A female mountain bluebird, common summer resident.* TOM ULRICH *Right: Blue grouse lives year-round in coniferous forests.* JESS LEE

years there has been some success in bringing back fisheries on such streams as the lower Clearwater and upper Salmon, but proposed increases in logging on National Forest lands, as well as continued degradation of riparian zones by livestock, threaten to thwart all efforts. Many mountain lakes and streams have populations of cutthroat, lake, brown, Dolly Varden, brook, rainbow and golden trout.

There is a bias obvious in the species I have chosen to highlight here. I have concentrated on the larger mammals because these wildlife species are the ones most people will see and readily identify, not because they are more

important or interesting than, say, chipmunks or flying squirrels. Each species of Idaho's wildlife is essential for the smooth ecological working of the whole, and the loss of one creates problems for others. Compared to those of other states, Idaho's wildlife has fared well, but nearly every species has suffered some kind of habitat destruction, persecution or overhunting. But unlike less fortunate states, Idaho has been able to reverse or at least slow these downward trends. Wildlife is perhaps Idaho's most enduring natural resource and as my friend learned in New Zealand, without wildlife, mountains *are* just dead scenery.

6

NORTHERN IDAHO

Northern Idaho is blessed with many glacially-formed lakes, such as Lake Pend Oreille. JEFF GNASS

LAND OF LAKES

Whereas the mountains of southern Idaho offer spacious views, big sky, a sense of vastness and human isolation, northern Idaho with its rumpled, rolling, forested ranges is intimate and cozy—a comfortable environment where plants grow without coaxing, and nature seems to be within human dimensions. Thick, lush stands of cedar, hemlock, and fir swarm across both the valleys and ridges, and nestled among these forest-clad slopes are large lakes like Coeur d'Alene, Pend Oreille, Hayden and Priest, plus a host of smaller ponds and waterways. Indeed, the combination of forested mountains and blue lakes makes this portion of Idaho irresistible to many people and tourism is one of its major industries.

Northern Idaho's mountains are, on the average, the lowest in the state. The highest peaks are in the Selkirks and Cabinets, but even here few exceed 7,000'. The St. Joe, Coeur d'Alene and Purcell mountain ranges all average less than 6,000' in elevation; nevertheless, many of these mountains are still impressive since they rise steeply from low valleys which are often at less than 2,000'.

Two basic geological types dominate: the granitic rocks of the Kaniksu Batholith and the metasedimentary rocks of the Belt Supergroup. The Belt rocks are very ancient, formed more than one and a half billion years ago when a shallow sea lapped against the shoreline of the continental plate. On occasion the sea retreated enough to expose the wet mud, which dried and fossilized mud cracks, ripple marks and raindrops.

After deposition the Belt rocks were warped into folds and broken by faults. One of these major breaks is the Hope Fault, which the Clark Fork River follows from Montana into

Priest Lake is surrounded by the heavily forested Selkirk Mountains. RON SPOMER

Idaho. Another major displacement is the 300-mile Osborn Fault, which begins in western Montana and runs through Idaho to Coeur d'Alene. Interstate 90 and the Coeur d'Alene River follow the course of this fault. The St. Joe River follows a third fault to the south.

Mineralization is common along these major faults, and the giant silver deposits of the Coeur d'Alene mining district and other areas like the mines by Hope are located along these earth movements. Although Belt rocks dominate northern Idaho, there are several recent intrusions of granite. The Selkirk Mountains are one exposed surface, and portions of the Cabinet Mountains are also granite. In both cases, the overlying Belt rocks were eroded away, leaving behind the more durable granites.

The mountains of northern Idaho, more than those in any other part of the state, wear the scars of their encounter with Ice Age glaciers. During the height of the last Ice Age, nearly all of northern Idaho was covered with glacial ice. The ice not only occupied cirque basins and stream valleys, but also overrode the mountains, planing them smooth as if a giant sander had been taken to the land. The Selkirk and the Purcell mountains were almost entirely overridden by ice thousands of feet thick; only the highest peaks, like Smith Peak, Mt. Casey, Roman Nose and Scotchman Peak protruded above the grinding streams of ice.

The Purcell Trench, the large southern extension of the Rocky Mountain Trench (an 800-mile-long structural valley that extends from Sandpoint north into British Columbia) was completely buried with a huge glacial tongue, not once, but several times.

One of the later advances of glacial ice gouged out the Pend Oreille, Priest and other lake basins, then impounded the waters behind glacial moraine dams. Lake Pend Oreille is more than 1,100' in depth and U-shaped in profile; in essence, the lake was created in

37

The spectacular glaciated crest of the Selkirks is seen here at Chimney Rock. JERRY PAVIA

channel into the ice. Within a short time, perhaps only two days, the dam was destroyed and the waters of Lake Missoula roared across Idaho and eastern Washington with current velocities calculated to have been 45 miles per hour. The maximum rate of flow equalled 10 times the combined flow of all the world's rivers! The flood waters scoured eastern Washington down to bedrock, leaving giant plunge pools, basins and braided river channels in its wake. Grand Coulee in eastern Washington is just one remnant of these floods. Glacial Lake Missoula filled at least four times and perhaps as many as seven.

When the first whites arrived, several Indian groups were living in the northern part of what would later be known as Idaho. Near Bonner's Ferry on the Kootenai River lived the Kutenai tribe, a Plains people who seem to have moved into the area not long before, and adopted a fishing-hunting lifestyle. The Coeur d'Alenes and Kalispells, who were linguistically related to northwest Indian tribes, lived south of the Kutenai, from today's Sandpoint to the Coeur d'Alene area. All these tribes caught salmon, plentiful prior to the construction of dams along the Columbia. They also hunted, especially in winter, when deer and other species were trapped by snow and easy to approach on snowshoes. One visitor to the Coeur d'Alene Indians described how the Indians would kill deer without even bothering with weapons. They merely approached the animals floundering in deep snows, grabbed their heads and broke their necks, saving the expenditure of bullets. According to his account, over 600 deer were killed this way on one hunting trip.

The first white man into northern Idaho was David Thompson, of the Northwest Company of Montreal. He began business dealings with the Indians by Bonner's Ferry in 1808 and established Kullyspell House, a trading post, on the shores of Lake Pend Oreille in 1809. A few years later Kullyspell House was abandoned in favor of a new site called Spokane House—today the locale of a city of 200,000 in

much the same fashion as a coastal fiord. Interestingly, Lake Pend Oreille is some 291' higher than Kootenai Lake in Canada and the Purcell Trench slopes northward. Had it not been for recessional moraines north of Sandpoint that blocked the flow of water, the outlet of Pend Oreille would be north to Canada instead of west towards Priest River.

Near the close of the last ice age, giant glacial lakes were suddenly released and catastrophic floods that raced across eastern

Washington created the Channeled Scablands. During several of the Purcell glacial lobe advances, ice pushed up the Clark Fork Valley damming the Clark Fork River to creat Glacial Lake Missoula. At its highest level, the ancient lake had about half the volume of present-day Lake Michigan. Its surface stood at 4,150' above sea level, thus inundating most of the valleys of western Montana.

Eventually the lake began to spill over the lip of the dam and the stream quickly cut a

CARIBOU

A remnant population of no more than 30 woodland caribou (sometimes called mountain caribou) still roams the Selkirk Mountains in the very northwest portion of Idaho and adjacent portions of British Columbia. Several thousand woodland caribou are known to inhabit the mountains of British Columbia and Alberta, but the Selkirk group is the only known population in the United States. The animal is listed as an endangered species.

At one time the woodland caribou was widespread in Idaho, with individuals seen as far south as Elk City and McCall. Indiscriminate hunting of these tame and unwary animals eliminated them from most of their former habitat, except for inaccessible portions of the Selkirk Mountains.

The Selkirk animals show a distinct seasonal movement pattern. They spend January through mid-May on the highest ridges, where thin tree cover allows the sun to compact the snow, permitting travel on the hardened surface. Their primary winter food is arboreal lichen, the gray "moss" commonly draped on tree branches in this wet region. Lichens are a poor diet—low in protein, but high in carbohydrates—and barely provide sufficient energy for survival in this harsh environment.

In May caribou move to low elevations, particularly open areas like avalanche paths, recent burns and clearcuts. Here they feed on the lush new plant growth of valerian and huckleberry leaves. As summer progresses there is a gradual movement to higher spruce-fir forests where they stay until around November, when the first deep snows come.

These early snowfalls cover up caribou foods and the freshly-fallen uncompacted snow of the open forest makes travel laborious. The caribou seek refuge in old-growth cedar-hemlock forests whose dense canopies act as

A small herd of woodland caribou roams the higher Selkirk peaks near the Canadian border, surviving in winter on arboreal lichen. PHOTOS © GARY BRAASCH

umbrellas creating small yards where snow depth is shallow. This early-winter period is considered the most critical time of the year since travel is restricted and food generally sparse or unavailable. By January the snow has compacted enough to support the caribou's weight.

The woodland caribou is one of the slowest-breeding members of the deer family. Females do not breed until they are three and a half years old and then produce only one young per year. Within the Selkirk herd, reproduction has been particularly poor, perhaps as a result of inbreeding. Pregnant females display an odd behavior as birthing draws near in June—they abandon the warm, food-rich lowlands and move to the highest snowy ridges to calve. Some biologists believe the caribou avoids predators by this behavior, but these gains are balanced by a high mortality of calves that die from exposure on the snowy, windswept ridges.

The caribou population continues to dwindle as the old-growth cedar-hemlock forests critical for early winter survival are cut. The arboreal lichens necessary for caribou winter survival are available only on trees greater than 100 years old. Logging the subalpine spruce-fir forests eliminates this food source. In addition, the access provided by logging roads increases the problems associated with poaching and hunting. Each year caribou are mistakenly shot by hunters out for elk or deer.

One remedy is a proposed transplant of caribou from British Columbia to the Selkirks to augment the present herd and provide for greater genetic diversity. Biologists hope to increase the Selkirk herd to 100 or more individuals. If the Selkirk transplants prove successful, then other former caribou ranges in northern Idaho and northwest Montana may be targeted for the re-establishment of this wild symbol of the north.

the missionaries, including the St. Joe River, Priest Lake, and the town of St. Maries.

Gold rushes to the Coeur d'Alene region occurred in 1882, 1883, and 1884. But the future of this region lay in silver, not gold. Discoveries on the South Fork of the Coeur d'Alene River in 1884 and 1885 include the Tiger strike at Burke, the Morning at Mullan, the Polaris, the Sunshine, the Bunker Hill near Kellogg. Since 1884 the Coeur d'Alene mines have produced $4 billion worth of metals and in the late 1970s these mines were still producing 47 percent of the nation's silver.

One legacy of the mining era, the twin smelters at the Bunker Hill mine, for years spewed tons of pollutants into the air. A 1977 test of 1,000 Kellogg children showed that 88 percent had unsafe levels of lead in their blood. Lead deposits at a Kellogg elementary school were 160 times higher than the level regarded as safe. The contaminants also wrought havoc on the landscape, for which the barren, eroding mountainsides surrounding Kellogg are distressingly graphic evidence. Attempts to force the company into compliance with health and air pollution standards were roundly defeated by the citizens of Kellogg who, it seems, were more concerned about their jobs than the health of their children or the surrounding land. But their support of the company gave them only a few more years of work until the Bunker Hill Company closed down in 1981. As in Anaconda, Montana, the economic effects were disastrous; more than 2,000 people lost their jobs.

The original gold and silver rush to the area was followed by nearly as fevered a race for timber. Land could be staked and claimed under the 1878 Timber and Stone Act and the 1906 Forest Homestead Act in much the same way

eastern Washington.

Although fur trappers did venture through northern Idaho, it did not offer the prime beaver grounds that characterized southern Idaho. After the trapping era, the next substantial European venture was the establishment of Cataldo Mission along the Coeur d'Alene River. Father Pierre Jean De Smet visited the Coeur d'Alene tribe in 1842 and established the mission a short time after. Father Anthony Ravalli, who had worked at the St. Mary's Mission in Montana, came to Cataldo in 1850. Ravalli, along with several brothers and a group of Indians, built the present mission structure, which is the oldest standing building in Idaho. Many area names reflect the days of

ranchland could be homesteaded on the grasslands. Under either law, a person could claim 160 acres of timber land and eventually acquire it for as little as $2.50 an acre under the Timber and Stone Act and $1.25 an acre under the Forest Homestead Act. After gaining title to these timber stands, many people subsequently sold out to timber companies. In addition, many companies required workers to stake claims which were later signed over to their employers—as a requisite to keeping their jobs. In this way private timber companies came to control huge tracts of northern Idaho. In fact what is National Forest land in northern Idaho today is primarily real estate the timber companies thought was too steep or remote to be worth logging.

In the early days of logging, trains and, more commonly, river drives were used to move the cut timber to the mills. Today logs move by truck. On the Idaho Panhandle National Forests (the Coeur d'Alene, St. Joe, and Kaniksu, all under one administration), which cover most of northern Idaho, there are presently over 6,000 miles of logging roads. (Idaho has only 5,000 miles of paved roads in the entire state!) The Forest Service plans to construct another 7,000 miles during the next few decades at a cost of $500 million. Even without the new roads the Forest Service estimates that one fifth of the forest's watersheds, some 500,000 acres, have been damaged from sedimentation and other effects of roading.

Despite the prevalence of logging, a few mountain areas are still roadless and a number are proposed for wilderness designation, including the Mallard-Larkins in the St. Joe Mountains—an important elk and goat sanctuary—and Long Canyon in the Selkirks, where cedar-hemlock forests up to 500 years old

can be found. Salmo-Priest, in the extreme northwest corner of the state, and Scotchman's Peak in the Cabinet Mountains are two other proposed wildernesses.

Beside logging and tourism, the transfer of real estate itself is a major industry in this region. It seems that nearly everyone who passes through northern Idaho falls in love with the green valleys and forested mountains and a remarkably predictable scenario occurs over and over again. To people coming from areas where land prices are much higher, northern Idaho seems like the ideal place "to get back to the land" and many make a down payment on a five-acre plot. They go home, pack their belongings, gather up the kids and dog, and head back to Idaho to get away from the rat race. After buying a cow and planting a garden, they try somehow to survive in a region with chronically high unemployment—some by selling real estate to the next urban refugee. Then the first winter arrives, and the long dark nights and cloudy days begin to wear on the entire family. By next spring, they are packing up again and heading back to California, New York or wherever they came from, and the five acres are back on the market.

Yet the mountains keep drawing people back to northern Idaho and none are as enchanting as the Selkirks. Although most peaks are under 7,000', these mountains are rugged and austere on their ridges. The entire range was once overridden by glaciers, but after the retreat of the continental ice sheet, smaller cirque glaciers plucked away at valleys and mountain peaks to form a sculptured and ragged landscape. The canyons are clothed in dense forests typical of the Pacific Northwest with western hemlock, western red cedar, and Douglas fir.

The Selkirks are the refuge of the last population of woodland caribou in the United States. The caribou once ranged south in Idaho as far as Elk City. Overhunting, plus destruction of the old-growth forests—important to the caribou's winter survival—reduced the herd to an estimated 30 animals. These

Log raft along the shore of Coeur d'Alene Lake. GEORGE WUERTHNER

caribou range back and forth between Idaho and British Columbia along the Selkirk Crest. Only 30 individuals remain in the United States but there are plans to augment the herd with other caribou transplanted from British Columbia.

One of the most beautiful lakes in northern Idaho is 17.5-mile-long Priest Lake. This deep, glacially-carved lake is surrounded by a scenic backdrop of 7,000' peaks. The eastern shore of the lake is part of the state-owned Priest Lake State Forest. Controversy surrounds a proposed land trade between the state and a resort developer who wants to build condominiums, a ski area, three golf courses, swimming and tennis facilities, shops, restaurants, marinas, schools, an industrial park, aerial tramway, and other housing which could make the community the state's third largest city. Not everyone is pleased with the prospect of development on this scale and local opposition is considerable.

Across the Purcell Trench from the Selkirks and north of the Kootenai River are the Purcell Mountains, a southern extension of much higher Canadian mountains. Like the Selkirks, the Purcells are steep and heavily forested. The range was glaciated during the last ice age and there are numerous cirques, U-shaped valleys and other evidence of past glacial action. The highest peaks are just over 6,000'.

The Purcells and the Cabinets to the south are among the few places in Idaho where the grizzly bear can still be found. But that population is very small, probably no more than 50 individuals and perhaps less. If they are further isolated by new roading, development and human activity, these bears may suffer from a loss of genetic diversity as inbreeding occurs.

Besides grizzlies, the Purcells and Cabinets are home to mountain goat, moose, bighorn sheep, mountain lion, white tail and mule deer, mink, marten, weasel, beaver, bobcat, lynx, wolverine, fisher, coyote and a host of smaller mammals. Osprey and bald eagles are common along the waterways.

Lying between the Kootenai and Clark Fork rivers are the Cabinet Mountains, whose highest peak, Scotchman's Peak (7,009'), is part of a 100,000-acre wilderness proposed to span the Montana-Idaho borders. Part of the Cabinets are exposed granite, while the rest are primarily rocks of the Belt series. The rugged glaciated summits of the range are softened somewhat by the lush forest growth, but the higher reaches are predominantly bare rock broken by wet subalpine meadowlands. Here, as in a few other Idaho locations, mountain hemlock is a common timberline species. Roaming the heavily forested valleys and hillsides are a few grizzly bears—part of a dwindling population centered in the Montana part of the range.

South of the Cabinets between the Clark Fork Valley and the Coeur d'Alene Valley lie the Coeur d'Alene Mountains. A forested, rolling mountain range, this has been subjected to timber harvest and accessed by a spaghetti-like maze of logging roads. Besides the logging loss, a substantial percentage of the forest cover burned during the 1910 fires and is only now reforesting. One magnificent cedar grove that escaped the 1910 Burn is the 183-acre Settler's Grove on the upper portion of the West Fork of Eagle Creek, a Coeur d'Alene tributary. Some of the trees here are 30' in diameter and rival redwoods for beauty and size.

Placer mining was widespread in the Coeur d'Alene Mountains and a number of old mining communities such as Murray, Prichard, Eagle, Delta and Ferguson—most now little more than one or two standing buildings—are scattered along major gold-bearing drainages. Some of the streams, such as Prichard Creek, were ravaged by dredges and barren tailings cover entire valleys. Today active excavation is occurring in many of the former mining districts as miners rework the old tailings trying to recover gold that was missed earlier.

South of the Coeur d'Alene River are the

rolling ridges of the St. Joe Mountains, which are composed primarily of granites from the Idaho Batholith and Belt series rocks. Because of the overall low elevation of these mountains, little glaciation occurred and, like the Coeur d'Alenes, these have few truly dramatic mountains compared to the Sawtooth and other rugged ranges. Increased precipitation during the Ice Age helped to carve very deep river canyons out of the plateau-like mountains. Annual precipitation is still heavy; 24 inches falls at Potlatch, while 45 inches is common at Red Ives. Water continues its work on the St. Joes.

Another result of the glacial period was the formation of Coeur d'Alene Lake. The moraine from southward-moving glacier lobes blocked the St. Joe and Coeur d'Alene rivers and created the lake. Unfortunately, today parts of this beautiful lake are experiencing heavy pollution from leaking septic tanks of shoreline residences. In addition, tons of heavy metals were delivered into the lake from the Coeur d'Alene mines via the South Fork of the Coeur d'Alene River and water quality has steadily declined to the point where the native cutthroat trout fisheries are threatened.

The major drainage, the 133-mile-long St. Joe River, has 66.3 miles protected as Wild and Scenic. It once was one of the best trout fisheries in the world, with catches of seven- to nine-pound trout common. However, the St. Joe is the heart of the Idaho white pine country and with the coming of large-scale logging, water quality declined. Before truck transport, the St. Joe was a major log-drive route and hundreds of miles of log chutes and flumes in the surrounding mountains fed timber down into the river below. After the logs were collected, they were driven downstream during spring flood or during artificial floods created by surge-releases from dams constructed to hold water for this purpose.

Many people believe these northern Idaho mountains with their numerous lakes and rivers compose the most beautiful part of the state. And if the amount of tourism and the number of summer homes is any indication, few could argue with this assessment.

Left: Sunrise on the Purcells, as seen across the Kootenai National Wildlife Refuge.
Below: The Kootenai River flows through the Purcell Trench, part of an 800-mile-long structural fault running south from British Columbia. The Purcell Mountains are visible in the distance. JERRY PAVIA PHOTOS

7

WILDERNESS HEART

THE IDAHO BATHOLITH

In the center of any map of Idaho is a vast empty mountainous region, fringed by a handful of small settlements and skirted by a few roads. Except for U.S. Highway 12 over Lolo Pass, no paved roads cross this rough landscape. It is the largest single, relatively intact, chunk of roadless wild country left in the lower 48 states. The rugged, and for the most part inaccessible, mountains here include the Bitterroot, Salmon River and Clearwater Mountains, and all are underlain by the granitic rocks of the Idaho Batholith.

It was the emptiness, the lack of roads on the maps, that originally attracted me to Missoula, Montana, just east of the Idaho line. As a college-bound high school senior I followed different selection criteria in choosing a university for my undergraduate education: I wanted to be close to mountains, and the University of Montana in Missoula, on the eastern fringe of the Idaho Batholith, fulfilled this requirement beautifully. After graduating I remained here, not least of all because I can literally begin hiking out my back door and soon be swallowed up in the largest wilderness complex in the entire United States, south of Alaska. To me this is a comforting thought, even if I merely sit and look at the peaks.

A good percentage of these ranges have been given protection as designated wilderness. The Frank Church/River of No Return Wilderness, at 2.2 million acres (the same size as Yellowstone National Park), is presently the largest wilderness area in the lower 48. Just north of it lies the Selway-Bitterroot Wilderness, a 1.3-million acre preserve that includes a small portion of Montana and to the west, the 206,000-acre Gospel Hump Wilderness south of Elk City. Taken together these three areas

Above the headwaters of the North Fork of the Clearwater River, looking east over the northern portion of the Idaho Batholith. GEORGE WUERTHNER

44

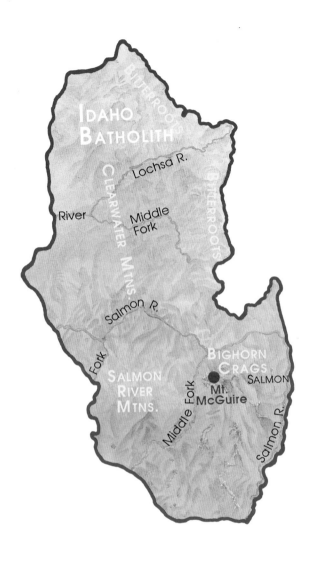

IDAHO
BATHOLITH

BITTERROOTS

Lochsa R.

CLEARWATER MTNS.

River

Middle
Fork

BITTERROOTS

Salmon R.

Fork

BIGHORN
CRAGS

SALMON
RIVER
MTNS.

Mt.
McGuire

SALMON

Middle Fork

Salmon R.

*The Salmon River's rapids-filled canyon
defied Lewis and Clark's efforts to find a route
down the river.* GEORGE WUERTHNER

Exposed granite at Blodgett Pass in the Bitterroots. The granite of Idaho's batholith was emplaced as molten rock when the North American continental plate overrode the Pacific plate. GEORGE WUERTHNER

comprise nearly all of Idaho's designated wilderness acreage.

The Idaho Batholith, which is the heart and soul of these ranges, was formed some 90 to 70 million years ago when molten rock was emplaced beneath the earth's surface as the North American plate moved westward like a conveyor belt, slowly overriding the Pacific plate below. The oldest magma was intruded along the western edge of the batholith and the youngest along the Montana border; exposed portions extend from near Boise and Sun Valley north toward Lookout Pass on Interstate 90. Although the granite rocks of the Boise Mountains, Payette Crest, Sawtooth and other south-central Idaho ranges are today recognized as part of the same basic batholithic formation, they have traditionally been treated as separate mountain ranges and so I will review them in other portions of the book.

The high mountains of the Idaho Batholith have discouraged human habitation for centuries. The Indians stayed on the fringes, venturing through only to hunt. Their old trails, such as the Lolo, followed the ridgetops and avoided the steep river canyons. The only Indians actually to inhabit the mountains year-round were the Sheepeater branch of the Shoshone tribe, who lived in very small bands along the Salmon River Canyon, subsisting on roots, berries, fish, and bighorn sheep—hence their name.

The first whites to enter the mountains of the Idaho Batholith were the members of the Lewis and Clark Expedition. Traveling the Indians' 158-mile-long Lolo Trail across the Bitterroot Mountains in 1805, the Expedition found the going extremely difficult as Clark recorded in his journal after the first day: "... the road through this hilley countery is verry bad passing over hills and thro' steep hollows, over falling timber, etc.... Crossed a mountain 8 miles without water and encamped on a hill side on the creek after descending a long steep mountain." But the trail got no better, in fact it worsened as wet snow added to their misery. On top of the difficult traveling, they could find no game along the route and were forced to kill and eat several of their horses. On September 22 the expedition floundered out of the mountains onto the Weippe Prairie where they met a group of Nez Perce Indians, who fed them buffalo meat, and dried roots and berries.

After the Lewis and Clark Expedition passed through the area, few other whites entered these rugged mountains until gold was discovered in Idaho. The first strike was made in 1860 by E.D. Pierce (the town of Pierce is named for him) along the western edge of the batholith in the Clearwater Mountains, within the boundaries of the Nez Perce Indian Reservation. The reservation had been closed to any prospecting, but once Pierce found traces of gold, the rush was on. By the following June several thousand miners had illegally entered the reservation and two years after Pierce's initial discovery Shoshone County had the largest population in Washington Territory (of which Idaho was still a part).

Once they transgressed the reservation borders, prospectors began to spread throughout central Idaho in search of new gold strikes. In May of 1861, gold was discovered on the South Fork of the Clearwater and Elk City sprang up around these placer deposits. New discoveries occurred all summer as miners raced ahead of each other trying to be the first to work a new area. In September, Florence Basin was discovered 40 miles south of Elk City and by the following spring more than 10,000 miners had journeyed to the strike. All this took place in spite of the fact that prospecting on the reservation was still illegal. Some miners were making between $100 and $1,000 a day and more than $9.6 million in gold came out of the Florence deposits in this one big year. More placer deposits were discovered along the south and southeastern margin of the batholith at Leesburg near Salmon in 1866 and at Loon Creek near Challis in 1869.

The entire time thousands of miners were trespassing on the Nez Perce Reservation, the Indians maintained a restrained attitude, but the tension on both sides grew until the spring

Columbia River basalts cover the batholith's western edge, in the Clearwater Mountains near Kooskia. GEORGE WUERTHNER

of 1877. General Howard gave Chief Joseph, Chief White Bird, and other tribal leaders an ultimatum, either move voluntarily or be forcefully escorted to a new reservation in northern Idaho. Unwilling to risk war, the leaders reluctantly agreed to settle on the new reservation. Within Indian society, however, no leader has absolute control of tribal members and on June 14, 1877, some of the younger members of White Bird's band, who'd had enough of broken treaties, attacked white settlers along the Salmon River. When the cavalry skirmished with the Indians on June 17 on White Bird Creek, the so-called Nez Perce War began. A month later another battle on the Clearwater forced the Indians to abandon Idaho and flee toward Montana over the same Lolo Trail that had brought Lewis and Clark into the state some 72 years before. The Indians fought several more battles while working their way across Montana until they reached the Bearpaw Mountains by the Canadian border. Here, weary in body and spirit, Joseph surrendered along with 79 men and 352 women and children. White Bird escaped to Canada

with 98 men and about 200 women and children. The Nez Perce War was over.

The Salmon River Mountains are the batholith's highest. They are bounded on the north by the Salmon River Breaks and on the south by towns such as Stanley, Challis and Salmon. The South Fork of the Salmon River forms the western boundary. Some of the higher peaks are Twin Peaks (10,340'), Sleeping Deer Mountain (9,800'), Big Baldy (9,722') and Mt. McGuire (l0,052'). A large percentage of this range was set aside as the Idaho Primitive Area, which with some boundary adjustments became the 2.2-million-acre Frank Church/River of No Return Wilderness in 1980. Except for the Big Horn Crags, most of this vast area is lightly traveled even though accessible by an excellent trail system. In addition some 24 primitive airstrips lace the back country, providing access to remote dude ranches, Forest Service ranger stations and outfitter camps. Several air taxis in Challis, Salmon and McCall specialize in "bush air service" similar to that found in Alaska.

Within the Salmon River Mountains there

Top: The Salmon River (seen here near Ellis) and its sources dissect an uplifted plateau, defining the Salmon River Mountains. GEORGE WUERTHNER
Below: Launch site for floats down the Middle Fork of the Salmon River. ERWIN AND PEGGY BAUER

are few alpine areas, and much of the terrain, outside of the river canyons, is forested and undulating. For example, the huge Chamberlain Basin in the center of these mountains is a relatively flat, high plateau, dotted with meadows and surrounded by the deep canyons of the South Fork and main Salmon rivers. These gorges were cut mainly during the last 1 million years, particularly during the latter part of the Ice Age when melt waters of the glaciers swelled the volume and hence the cutting power of the rivers.

Above 7,500' the country displays cirque basins, U-shaped valleys and other glacial landforms; one of the most spectacular examples of glaciation within the Salmon River Mountains can be found in a small sub-range, the Big Horn Crags.

The Salmon River Mountains contributed their share to Idaho's mining history. Gold was taken out of placers at Shoup, Big Creek, Leesburg, Yankee Fork and Loon Creek. Silver

THE 1910 BURN

Just 20 years after the Nez Perce war, in 1897, most of the timbered portions of Idaho's mountains were included in the newly created forest reserve system. In 1905 the system came under the control of a new agency—the Forest Service. Besides controlling overgrazing and indiscriminate logging, the new agency's primary role was to combat forest fires. Just five years after its creation the Forest Service's firefighting abilities were sorely tested as it strove to control flames that eventually burned over 3 million acres. The fires are known collectively as the 1910 Burn, although they were in fact separate blazes that raged across Idaho and adjacent parts of Montana.

The spring of 1910 was very dry and, by July, lightning had started small fires throughout the northern Rockies. With few trails, and fewer roads, the agency was hard pressed to control any blazes and by August the fires were so widespread that President Taft authorized the use of the army for fire fighting. On August 20, gale-force winds whipped fires from the Canadian border south to Salmon in a holocaust that filled the sky with so much smoke that darkness came by four in the afternoon. The heat of the conflagration created huge convection currents generating their own winds and propelling great swirling masses of flames across valleys and from peak to peak. A third of the town of Wallace burned down and many other communities were threatened. Thousands fled, riding special trains to Missoula and Spokane. The flames were finally quenched by heavy rain on August 31. The human death toll was 85 people, including 78 fire fighters.

Although the charred snags of the old 1910 Burn can still be seen in many places today, the land quickly recovered and a few years after the fire, brush began to cloak the fire-scarred slopes. By 1940, some 30 years after the fire, the

wild fastness of the 1910 Burn was the best elk habitat in the state and an estimated 40,000 elk roamed the Clearwater National Forest alone. With continued fire suppression, much of this brush that had provided elk with excellent forage began to revert to coniferous forest—a less nutritious food—and elk numbers declined.

Today there is a growing awareness of the natural role of fire in forest ecosystems and events like the 1910 Burn are not seen as tragic, except, of course, in the occasional loss of human life. Within the Selway-Bitterroot Wilderness and other selected areas throughout the west, managers are experimenting with a new "let burn" policy where naturally ignited fires are allowed to burn uncontrolled if certain pre-determined environmental conditions are met. In places like the Selway, this may mean that there will be more elk as fires once again create the brushy habitat so essential to elk reproduction and survival. More importantly, wild fires are part of the natural functioning of the ecosystem and essential for a healthy forest. Frequent fires reduce the possibility of large conflagrations by eliminating fuel accumulations. They also reduce the severity of insect attacks by killing larvae, and the periodic thinning of young saplings by low-level ground fires creates open, park-like stands.

Left: Wallace in 1910, just after the Great Burn. NEGATIVE NO. 8-X478, BARNARD STOCKBRIDGE COLLECTION, UNIVERSITY OF IDAHO LIBRARY
Above: A snag remaining from the 1910 burn, on a ridge near Hoodoo Pass on the Idaho-Montana border. GEORGE WUERTHNER

was mined at Greyhound, Seafoam, and Bay-horse. At Thompson Creek along the Salmon River a huge molybdenum deposit was discovered by Cyprus Mining Corporation in the late 1960s, but was not developed until the 1980s. Hundreds of workers flooded into Challis, the nearest community, and the usual problems associated with a boom economy developed, including rising crime, a lack of housing and of adequent schools. After a few years of intense activity, the price of molybdenum fell and mining declined somewhat; its activity fluctuates with mineral prices. A similar drop in mineral prices doomed cobalt mining along Panther Creek just east of the Crags, part of the Frank Church/River of No Return Wilderness 39,000-acre Special Mining Management Area. The town of Cobalt boomed for a short time in the early 1980s until the market went soft. It now sits, essentially a ghost town, waiting for the next upsurge in cobalt prices.

The 425-mile Salmon River, which drains the mountains of the same name, is the longest river in the nation that begins and flows entirely within one state. Several stretches of the Salmon have been officially designated Wild and Scenic, including 96 miles of the Middle Fork, and 125 miles of the main Salmon. Beginning at an elevation of more than 8,000' in the upper Stanley Valley, the Salmon drops to 905' where it enters the Snake River near Lewiston. Along the 79-mile course through the rugged Salmon River gorge in the center of the Frank Church/River of No Return Wilderness, the river drops an average of 12' per mile, and in many places the canyon is over one mile deep—attributes that make it one of the most popular whitewater float trips in the west.

Along the western edge of the Salmon River Mountains is the South Fork of the Salmon River. The South Fork was at one time the most important chinook salmon spawning area in the entire Columbia River system, contributing 55 percent of the drainage's summer chinook population. An estimated 50,000 salmon were produced annually, and over 10,000 returned to spawn. Between 1950 and 1965 much of the

At Bayhorse in the Salmon River Mountains, along the edge of the Idaho batholith. JAMES K. MORGAN

South Fork drainage was logged and over 800 miles of logging roads were constructed on highly erodable soils. The resulting sedimentation from roads and unstable slopes destroyed the fisheries. Only 300 salmon now return to the river—and this is an improvement over the last decade! The South Fork is slowly healing, and could once again be a major salmon fishery. Its revival is uncertain, however, as the Payette National Forest proposes renewed logging for the drainage.

The Salmon River Mountains harbor dozens of species that depend on wilderness: they are harmed by human disturbance of their habitats or the heavy hunting pressure that comes with road networks. For example, more bighorn sheep are found here than anywhere else in Idaho partly because the rugged canyons restrict the ability of domestic livestock to graze wild sheep habitat. Populations include an estimated 250 bighorns on Panther Creek, 175 on Morgan Creek, 600 along the Middle Fork, and another 200 along the main Salmon below the town of North Fork. A lack of roads means elk are disturbed less and, as a consequence, some of Idaho's larger herds are found here, including some 1,000 to 1,200 that roam the Salmon River Breaks country and another 600 to 800 in the Panther Creek area. Other large herds are scattered throughout the mountains, including the

Chamberlain Basin. Mule deer, mountain lions, black bears, and goats are also common in their respective habitats within these mountains.

Many of the less common species like wolverine, lynx and wolves are wilderness-dependent in that they need large areas of undisturbed habitat simply to avoid conflict or contact with humans. Other species like the boreal owl, a bird only recently discovered to be breeding in these mountains, are dependent upon hollow nest cavities found in old-growth timber, a habitat rapidly disappearing outside of formal wilderness because of the logging of mature timber stands.

Lying north of the Salmon River Mountains are the Bitterroot Mountains which, if you include the Beaverhead Mountains as a southern extension of the range as many geographers do, form the longest mountain range in the lower 48 states. Even without including the Beaverhead, the Bitterroot are an impressive range stretching from Lost Trail Pass to Lookout Pass on Interstate 90. The highest summits in this section are along the Montana-Idaho divide and include Watchtower Peak (8,780'), and Ranger Peak (8,819'). Just a few miles east of the state line in Montana are peaks a thousand feet or more higher, such as 10,211' Trapper Peak. Over 1.3 million acres of the central Bitterroot Mountains are part of the Selway-Bitterroot Wilderness, which, until creation of the Frank Church/River of No Return Wilderness, was the largest designated wilderness in the lower 48 states.

The Bitterroots are composed almost entirely of granites, quartz monzonites and gneiss. The higher peaks of these mountains were extensively glaciated, particularly those along the crest forming the Idaho-Montana border. The Selway Crags are another outlying, heavily glaciated granite mass west of the main divide.

Between Lolo Pass and Lookout Pass are the northern reaches of the Bitterroot Mountains. Lower, and less rugged than the main crest to the south, this area nevertheless experienced glaciation and is dotted with cirque lakes and U-shaped valleys. Much of the high country

Looking across the Salmon River Mountains toward the Middle Fork of the Salmon River. GEORGE WUERTHNER

The crest of the granitic Bitterroots (seen here above Blodgett Lake on the Idaho-Montana border) always has presented a rugged barrier to human travel. Most old trails followed the ridgelines. GEORGE WUERTHNER

In this part of Idaho one encounters some tree species not found to the south in the state. Many are Pacific coast disjunct species whose centers of distribution are to the west in the Cascades, including the previously mentioned western red cedar, the large white blossomed Pacific dogwood and sword fern. On the highest peaks it is possible to find the mountain hemlock, whose main range lies from the Sierras in California north to Alaska. In addition, in the old burns one will find paper birch, a common boreal forest species found across the north from New England to Alaska. In the highest parts of the Bitterroot on rocky ridges grows alpine larch, a hardy species found only in a very restricted area of the northern Rockies and northern Cascades. Alpine larch needles turn gold in autumn, and drop off, leaving the branches bare all winter.

The Bitterroot Mountains are drained primarily by the Selway and Lochsa rivers, of which 96 miles of the Selway and 65 miles of the Lochsa are designated Wild and Scenic Rivers. Both were once major salmon- and steelhead-producing rivers. Efforts to re-establish runs have been hampered by downstream dams and the continued sedimentation of headwater drainages and tributaries by new logging. For example, White Sand Creek, a Lochsa tributary which has the potential to produce 27 percent of the steelhead and 26 percent of the chinook salmon on the Clearwater National Forest, is scheduled to be logged within the next few years.

The Lochsa and Selway salmon runs were important high protein food sources to grizzlies. William Wright, a naturalist and hunter in the late 1800s, recounts watching grizzlies fish for salmon along these rivers much as they do in Alaska today. Some people speculate that the demise of grizzlies within the Selway ecosystem is the result of losing the salmon as a food source. No doubt, with a decline in these runs birth rates dropped, along with the survival rates of the cubs born. This, combined with hunting, may have done in the Bitterroot grizzly. Grizzlies survived in the range until

was burned in the 1910 fires and has not reforested; instead, a fire-induced alpine area lies at a much lower elevation than would be expected at this latitude.

The Bitterroot are influenced more by the Pacific Maritime climate than areas farther south, and since they are the highest peaks air masses encounter after crossing the Cascades in Washington, precipitation is heavy. In the winter months clouds cover the range 80 to 90 percent of the time. A gradation in precipitation occurs, with the driest areas to the south

near the Salmon River and a gradual increase in moisture as one moves north, until annual precipitation approaches 80 or more inches. Where fires have not cleared the hillsides, thick forests of cedar, western larch, Douglas fir, western white pine, and in the drier areas, stands of ponderosa pine, blanket the hillsides. Higher up one finds lodgepole pine, subalpine fir, mountain hemlock and whitebark pine. Common understory plants include beargrass, huckleberry, ninebark, oceanspray, redstem ceanothus, snowberry, and thimbleberry.

the 1940s when the last bear was killed. Reports of grizzlies still filter out of these mountains each summer, however, giving rise to speculation that at least a few of the bruins wander down into the Bitterroot from grizzly habitat farther north.

With the loss of the grizzly, black bear populations increased, with some 1,200 black bears thought to exist on the Clearwater National Forest alone. In addition to these animals, the Bitterroot Mountains are inhabited by wolverine, marten, lynx, and even a few roaming wolves. Mountain goats occur in all the high peaks and moose are widely distributed throughout the range. The Bitterroot elk herd is one of the largest in the nation and annually attracts hunters from around the world, who support a large outfitting industry in the region.

During the late 1800s and early 1900s no roads and few trails cut across the rugged Bitterroot and they were among the wildest and most remote mountains in the west. Much of the western side of the mountains was more accessible from Montana than from any Idaho community. As a result, many Montana trappers and hunters crossed the Bitterroot Divide and worked illegally in Idaho so that locals called the area just west of the state line "Lapland," where "Montana lapped over into Idaho." Because of the vastness of the roadless region, game wardens and other officials were frequently thwarted in their efforts to catch wrongdoers.

Although a good percentage of the central Bitterroot lies within the Selway-Bitterroot Wilderness, much of the northern part of the range, along with adjacent areas of the Clearwater Mountains, remains the focus of debate between pro- and anti-wilderness factions. Several large roadless areas in the upper North Fork of the Clearwater, such as the Great Burn, Moose Mountain, Bighorn-Weitas, Sheep Mountain and Mallard-Larkin, comprise 600,000 acres of potential wilderness. Several dirt roads could be closed to join these areas into

Tall dead snags along the Lochsa River, in the Bitterroots, are evidence of the 1910 Burn. JEFF GNASS

Spring along the South Fork of the Clearwater River near Grangeville. GEORGE WUERTHNER

one large unit, but at this time political support for such closures, much less wilderness designation, is almost completely lacking in Idaho's congressional delegation.

The Clearwater Mountains lie west of the Bitterroot Mountains and are, over all, much lower. Hills and ridges run into each other and there is no agreement as to where one mountain range ends and the next begins. These mountains derive their name from the Clearwater River and its tributaries that flow from the range. The Clearwater, like the Salmon River Mountains to the south, are primarily a high rolling plateau dotted by an occasional higher peak or promontory, carved by deeply incised river canyons. As with the Bitterroot, most of these mountains are composed of granites, quartz monzonite, schist and gneiss. On the extreme eastern edge of the mountains by Grangeville, Kooskia and Orofino and farther north, basalt flows have flooded the lower valleys and now cover these other rocks. Over most of the range, the highest peaks barely exceed 8,000′. Nevertheless, because of the heavy annual precipitation, particularly in the northern portions of these mountains, timberline is lower and many peaks above 7,000′ have alpine areas. In addition, because of the higher precipitation characteristic of these mountains glaciation occurred at a lower elevation than farther south and many mountains above 5,000′ have been glaciated.

The heavy precipitation and generally low elevation promote tree growth and, as might be expected, timber harvest dominates the economies of nearby towns like Elk City, Pierce, Weippe and Kooskia. These communities were the focus of much of the early logging industry in Idaho, which centered on the harvest of western white pine. In this region western white pine is the most abundant species and at one time old-growth trees towered over the canyons and slopes of the Clearwater Mountains and St. Joe Mountains to the north. These old-growth trees were frequently 200′ in height

54

Sword and maidenhair fern, with moss, along Green Creek in the Clearwaters. GEORGE WUERTHNER

and 10' or more in diameter. Few of these forest giants remain any more; in what must surely be an ignoble end, many of these huge western white pine were cut to produce matchsticks. And in more recent years, white pine blister rust, accidentally introduced from Europe and deadly to older pine, has killed many of these forest titans.

Much of the Clearwater Mountains has been given over to logging, but some rather large roadless areas remain. The Meadow Creek drainage on the Nez Perce National Forest near Elk City is a major steelhead-spawning tributary of the Selway River and a proposed 200,000-acre addition to the existing Selway-Bitterroot Wilderness. In 1985 roads were built into Meadow Creek's headwaters to access timber, even though the Forest Service's own evaluation stated that logging the fragile, granitic slopes would harm the Meadow Creek fisheries. In addition, many local loggers opposed the sale since the trees will have to be hauled over 100 miles to mills, making it unprofitable to harvest even with government subsidy. Nevertheless, the roading and cutting continue unabated.   Other large roadless areas in the Clearwater Mountains area, which conservationists propose for partial or total wilderness protection, include the 52,000-acre Grandmother Mountain-Pichot Butte area, the 400,000-acre Mallard Larkin-Sheep Mountain area, and 60,000-acre Fish-Hungry Creek area. Just how much of these areas, if any, remain roadless 40 or 50 years from now, depends a great deal upon decisions made today.

The mountains of the Idaho Batholith are not Idaho's highest, nor even most majestic, but they are easily the wildest country left in the lower 48 states. And for that reason alone they will continue to have an allure and appeal to Idahoans and the nation. As author Wallace Stegner once wrote, wilderness constitutes "the geography of hope" and these wild mountains of the Idaho Batholith hold the promise for Idaho's future and a key to its past.

8

SAWTOOTH COUNTRY

The ruggest crest of the Sawtooths reflects the erosive power of the glaciers that once covered this range, which was first proposed for protected status in 1916 and was designated as wilderness in 1972. GEORGE WUERTHNER

Tucked away in central Idaho just north of the Snake River Plain and south of the Salmon River are Idaho's most famous mountains, the Sawtooth, and a number of equally majestic ranges like the Boulder, Pioneer, White Cloud and Smoky mountains. In recognition of its nationally known scenic splendor, a good percentage of the region is now part of the Sawtooth National Recreation Area (NRA)—after years of effort to gain protected status for these mountains.

Public interest in the Sawtooth was first initiated in 1911, when some Idaho clubwomen endorsed a plan to establish a Sawtooth National Park. Additional bills to afford some kind of special designation were introduced in Congress in 1916, 1935, 1960 and 1963. Finally, in 1972, a 754,000-acre Sawtooth National Recreation Area was created, its core the 216,000-acre Sawtooth Wilderness with nearly 300 lakes and 50 peaks over 10,000'.

Wilderness or not, recreation is the economic lifeblood of this area. Sun Valley adjacent to the old mining town of Ketchum was the first ski resort in the United States, brainchild of Averill Harriman, chairman of the board for the Union Pacific Railroad, who became fascinated with skiing after observing the sport in the European Alps. After considering potential resort sites at Mt. Rainier, Yosemite, the San Bernardino Mountains, the Wasatch Mountains and Jackson Hole, he chose Ketchum as the ideal location.

In 1937 the Union Pacific bought a 3,888-acre ranch near Ketchum and began construction of an elaborate lodge and ski slopes on Dollar and Proctor Mountain. A Union Pacific engineer, James Curran, built the world's first chair lifts—fashioned after ore-bucket lifts he had seen in use in South American mines; he simply replaced the bucket with a chair. The railroad then hired Steve Hannagan, a man who had

The town of Stanley sits below the rugged Sawtooth Mountains. JEFF GNASS

promoted Miami Beach as a resort, to help sell the idea of Sun Valley to the American public. It was Hannagan who decided to give the new complex the optimistic name of "Sun Valley."

One of the resort's earliest celebrities was Ernest Hemingway, who first visited Sun Valley in 1939. While there he wrote a portion of his novel, *For Whom the Bell Tolls*. After living in a number of other countries he eventually returned to Ketchum-Sun Valley for the rest of his life.

Long before Sun Valley was even an idea in Averill Harriman's mind, the Wood River Valley was a major Indian route between the upper Salmon River valley and the Camas Prairies by Fairfield. Deep trails were worn over the passes and down the river. Trappers and other early travelers used these same routes in the early 1800s and, while passing down the Wood River in 1834, naturalist John Townsend noted, "It [the Wood River] contains

a great abundance of beaver, their recent dams being seen in great numbers."

Except for fur brigades that worked the beaver-rich Wood River, trappers spent little time in these game-poor mountains; they usually passed through on their way to richer hunting grounds. Although bighorn sheep were abundant in the upper reaches of the East Fork of the Salmon and Big Lost River valleys, other wildlife—bison for example—were scarcer here than in other areas. But today all of these ranges have populous herds of elk, goats and deer while in other parts of the state human developments have eliminated a large percentage of wildlife habitat. In some locations there are bighorn sheep and antelope. The wolverine, a very rare animal in Idaho, has been sighted in all the Sawtooth ranges, and the Sawtooth NRA may well be its stronghold in the state. Grizzlies were eliminated by stockmen long ago; black bears persist, if in limited numbers.

Even though many wildlife species have recovered from past declines, some instinctive or learned animal traditions may have been lost forever. For example, elk once migrated from the Wood River Valley out to the lower Snake River Plain for the winters. But elk were exterminated from the Wood River by miners and later, re-introduced animals lacked the tradition of migration. Hence they winter in the high, snow-covered valleys and frequently starve.

After the trapping era, the region was given back primarily to Indian use and travel. The first lasting white settlement occurred after minerals were discovered in the Wood River valley around the 1880s. Towns that owe their existence to the mining era include Bellevue, Hailey and Ketchum. Between 1880 and 1889 the Wood River area was Idaho's leading mineral-producing region; some $60 million

Castle Peak, the highest peak in the White Cloud Mountains, was the site of a controversial proposed open-pit mine. The area now is part of the Sawtooth National Recreation Area, but still open to mining.
HOWIE WOLKE

worth of gold, lead and silver were taken from area mines.

About the same time that the Wood River mines came into operation, other mineral discoveries in the Stanley Basin created the towns of Vienna and Sawtooth City. A toll road was constructed over Trail Creek summit in 1884, connecting Ketchum with Challis and Bayhorse. Huge wagonloads of ore were delivered over this road to smelters in the Wood River Valley. All this activity brought prosperity to the Wood River communities; Bellevue had three papers, Hailey two. These towns also had the first telephones and electric lights in Idaho. But the good times were short-lived and crashes in silver prices in 1888 and 1892 brought an end to big-time mining in this region.

The mining was replaced by the sheep industry. Basque sheepherders began to drive their herds into the high country of the Boulder, Sawtooth and Pioneer mountains and by the 1920s Ketchum could boost that it was the largest sheep and lamb shipping station in the United States.

A limited amount of ranching still occurs in the high valleys surrounding these mountains, and grazing occurs on the Forest Service lands in summer, but recreation now dominates the area. People come to backpack, ski, float rivers, fish, hunt, rockhound, camp and simply enjoy the tremendous mountain scenery. In the long run, much more gold will be taken from tourist pockets than ever was hauled out of the mines or garnered from sheep fleeces.

Although many of the higher reaches of these mountains are forested with Douglas fir, lodgepole pine, Englemann spruce, aspen, subalpine fir, whitebark pine and limber pine, the slow growth at these elevations has discouraged a timber industry. There are no western larch, western white pine, western cedar and other trees common just a few hundred miles to the north. Ponderosa pine grows along some of the lower river valleys, such as the South Fork of the Payette and lower Salmon, but is otherwise absent from these ranges.

There are many large tree-fringed meadows and when the wildflowers are in bloom, they appear like colored puddles of blue, pink or gold. I have seen blue camas—whose bulb was eagerly sought by Indian tribes of the northern Rockies—growing so profusely that I've mistaken moist meadows of the Stanley Basin for ponds of blue water. Other flowers common to the area are shooting star, fireweed, elephanthead, scrubby cinquefoil, and mariposa.

Of all these mountains, the Sawtooth command particular attention and part of the Sawtooths' attraction can be attributed to its geological history. The granites that comprise the Sawtooth Mountains were formed 50 million years ago; overlying rocks that covered the batholith were removed by erosion; this metamorphosed cap rock still can be seen crowning Thompson Peak by Stanley. The Challis volcanics were extruded over this erosional surface some 25 million years ago and these too were later eroded away. About 1 million years ago—very recently in geological terms—these mountains were uplifted along two major faults: the Montezuma fault near Atlanta and the Sawtooth fault along the northeast margin of the range. The rising batholith was then exposed to additional erosion and the many closely spaced joints or cracks common to this particular granite allowed weathering of serrated ridges, giving the mountains their name.

The effects of glaciation are evident everywhere. Giant ice tongues scooped out basins and later, water backed up behind moraine dams to fill Redfish, Alturis, Petit and other large lakes. One glacial tongue extended

Mount Heyburn reflected in Little Redfish Lake, a moraine-dammed lake. The low grass-covered hill on the right is a lateral morain left by the glacier that created Little Redfish and Redfish lakes. JEFF GNASS

across the Stanley Valley where it narrows just south of today's Stanley, where Redfish Lake drains into the Salmon River, and blocked the river to form a large glacial lake. The bottom of this former lake can be seen as the smooth, flat valley of the Stanley Basin. Most of the low, forested hills seen at canyon mouths are glacial moraines. The mixture of gravel and boulders in the moraines is highly permeable and favors the growth of deep-rooted plants like trees, while the fine-particled soils in the valleys favor the growth of grasses. Besides the larger lakes, some 300 alpine cirque lakes adorn the high country. U-shaped valleys, horns, aretes, and cols are to be seen everywhere and even a few remnant glaciers lie in high basins on Thompson Peak in the upper Goat Creek valley.

Although a number of different trapping parties entered the Stanley Basin, none stayed long for there were few beaver. The high mountain valley with its deep snows was not the best wildlife habitat for big-game species like elk and deer and, even today, these animals are rather uncommon. But higher up in the Sawtooth, where steep terrain and winds keep the ground snow-free, one of Idaho's largest goat herds is found.

The most unique wildlife are the anadromous fish in the upper Salmon River. Redfish Lake gets its name from the large number of sockeye salmon that once spawned here. The 800-mile spawning runs were the longest recorded for sockeye salmon in the world, but the construction of the Sunbeam Dam in 1910 destroyed most of the run. The dam was dynamited in 1934, allowing the passage of some salmon, but only 20 to 30 adult sockeyes still make it back to Redfish Lake to spawn each fall.

Chinook or king salmon are much larger than

Canyon Creek, a tributary of the South Fork of the Payette, is among the headwaters of several major rivers that rise in the Sawtooths, including the Salmon and Middle Fork of the Boise. GEORGE WUERTHNER

PHOTO COURTESY OF THE IDAHO STATESMAN

Frank Church at Boy Sout Jamboree, 1973

FRANK CHURCH

Senator Frank Church represented the people of Idaho and, on some concerns, the nation as a whole for more than a quarter century. He was a strong supporter of conservation efforts and helped to draft both the 1964 Wilderness Act and the 1968 Wild and Scenic Rivers Act. In addition, he wrote the 1972 bill establishing the Sawtooth National Recreation Area and helped create the Hells Canyon National Recreation Area in 1975. Through his leadership, the largest wilderness area in the lower 48 states—the 2.2-million-acre River of No Return Wilderness—was established. After his death in 1984, the name was changed to the Frank Church/River of No Return Wilderness to honor his accomplishments.

These conservation measures were not always popular with many Idahoans and Church endured some insults such as being hung in effigy by wilderness opponents during hearings for the Gospel Hump Wilderness. He voluntarily took a personal loss when the Sawtooth National Recreation Area was created: Church and his wife Bethine gave up the family ranch where they had been married in 1947, rather than keep an inholding on the NRA. His defense of Idaho's natural resources for long-term economic and ecological stability rather than short-term exploitation probably cost him re-election in 1980. It is a fitting epitaph to have one of the great wild places left in America, the Frank Church/River of No Return Wilderness, named after one who worked diligently for its protection.

sockeyes—the largest caught in Alaska weigh more than 100 pounds. Chinook ascend the river earlier in the summer than the fall-spawning sockeye, when more water pours over the remains of the Sunbeam Dam. Consequently more of them arrive at their spawning grounds. But they have their problems as well. Overgrazing and destruction of riparian habitat by livestock have severely impacted the small feeder streams where young salmon are hatched and reared. Sedimentation from logging activity also plays a part in the decline of salmon fisheries, although less so here than in areas where timber harvest is greater. In addition, treaty rights allow Indians to spear fish in the shallow-water spawning streams. Because so few fish reach these tributaries, this assault on their population can have a severe impact.

To the east of the Sawtooth are the White Cloud Mountains culminating in 11,815' Castle Peak. These mountains became the center of controversy in the late 1960s when a mining company proposed to develop an open pit molybdenum mine just below Castle Peak. The ensuing debate catapulted Cecil Andrus, who opposed the mining, into the governorship and later a position as Secretary of the Interior with the Carter administration. The mining has stopped, largely because of lack of demand, but the White Cloud and the nearby Boulder mountains are still the focus of intense debate over the merits of wilderness designation. Industry wants little or no wilderness, while conservation groups offer a number of proposals, for as much as 750,000

Frank Church helped establish the Sawtooth National Recreation Area, which includes the Sawtooths, seen here, and adjacent parts of the White Cloud, Boulder and Smoky Mountains. GEORGE WUERTHNER

covered with sagebrush and grass right up to the ridgetops. The open terrain is snow-covered in the winter, creating great natural ski slopes.

Moose are not native to this part of Idaho and the closest naturally occurring populations are in the Beaverhead Mountains near Salmon. In 1980 the Idaho Fish and Game introduced moose to the North Fork of the Big Lost River and, since then, these animals have increased steadily. One winter I found wolverine tracks on a snowy slope of the Boulder Mountains two miles east of the North Fork, by Deep Creek, but these mountains may not have a resident wolverine population as these wide-ranging animals are known to travel more than a hundred miles in a single week.

West of the White Knob Mountains and east of Wood River communities like Hailey and Ketchum, are the Pioneer Mountains. These have scores of peaks over 10,000', with Hyndman Peak at 12,009' the highest, while other high peaks include the Devil's Bedstead (11,100'), Big Black Dome (11,353'), Standhope Peak (11,700'), and Smiley Peak (11,508'). Taken as a group, this is Idaho's second highest mountain range. Aspen, lodgepole pine, Englemann spruce, Douglas fir, whitebark pine and subalpine fir are the primary tree species, but much of this country consists of open sagebrush-covered slopes extending to the tops of ridges. A large percentage of the Pioneer Range is still roadless and 182,000 acres are proposed for wilderness designation by Idaho conservation groups.

The Pioneer are composed of granites, metamorphosed sedimentary mudstones and Challis volcanics, and were extensively glaciated with many cirque lakes dotting the high country. Copper Basin, an open grassy mountain-rimmed valley at the head of the East Fork of the Big Lost River, is covered with hummocky glacial moraine.

acres of wilderness. That a proposal even of this size can be considered is a reflection of the area's significance.

The White Cloud Mountains get their name from a light-colored metamorphosed sandstone called quartzite: when viewed from a distance, they have the appearance of billowy clouds resting upon a green forested hillside. Remnants of past glaciation include nearly 100 alpine lakes and some stagnant ice patches above the Boulder Chain Lakes, half hidden beneath moraines.

The White Cloud are home to elk, deer, black bear, goats and a small herd of bighorn sheep. Salmon also spawn in the upper reaches of the East Fork of the Salmon River, while antelope occasionally are seen along its banks.

South of the White Cloud Mountains between the Lost River, Wood River and East Fork of the Salmon River drainages are the Boulder Mountains. Galena Peak (11,153'), Easley Peak (11,108'), and Silver Peak (11,112') reach impressive heights, but despite this, the Boulder Mountains are relatively unknown. Thousands of visitors drive by them yearly while climbing the road towards Galena Summit from the Ketchum-Sun Valley area, but most keep going north toward the spectacular Sawtooth. This is not to imply that the Boulder are dull-looking mountains. On the contrary, these peaks composed of Challis volcanics display the cirques and aretes of a glaciated range, though the eastern portion of the range near Bowery Peak and Sheep Mountain is more gentle and is

Falls Creek in the Pioneer Mountains.
GEORGE WUERTHNER

West of Ketchum and lying south of the Sawtooth are the virtually unknown Smoky Mountains. Mt. Baldy, location of the Sun Valley ski hill, is part of the eastern edge of this range. The range received its name during the 1880s from the smoke of forest fires that regularly plagued this area. The northern and western edges of the Smokies are composed of granites of the Sawtooth Batholith, while farther east the range is composed of Challis volcanics, limestones, quartzite, sandstone and conglomerate. Along the edge of the Sawtooth Batholith contact zone there are numerous hot springs, including Guyer, Warfield, Skillern, Lightfoot, Preis, Worswick and Clarendon. Glaciation was widespread and many of the higher peaks—including Norton Peak (10,336'), Baker Peak (10,117') and Big Peak (10,047')—all have their share of cirques, U-shaped valleys and alpine lakes.

Unlike the barren nearby Sawtooth, the Smoky Mountains contain some of the finest big-game habitat within the state. Big Smoky Creek is one of the few unroaded drainages left in south-central Idaho, and is an important elk habitat. Besides elk, the area is home to good populations of mule deer and mountain goat. Wolverines, very rare within the state, are found here in good numbers. Conservationists propose that 130,000 acres of the Smoky Mountains be protected as wilderness to give the elk, goats and wolverines a chance at survival with a minimal impact from man.

Even though these mountain ranges contain Idaho's most famous one, the Sawtooth, alongside it are almost unknown mountains like the Boulder. Almost anywhere besides Idaho, all these mountains would be renowned for their beauty, but these wild ranges harbor nameless valleys and quiet glades where the track of a deer is still more common than the footprint of a human.

9 BROAD VALLEY RANGES

I sometimes think I have a psychological fear of flat places. Kansas repels me. Florida is almost sure death. For a person with my affliction, Idaho's Broad Valley Rockies are a cure, for here lie Idaho's highest peaks. Not only are they the highest, but also they are little known.

My first sight of one range of these Broad Valley Rockies, the Lost River Range, left me feeling like I had stumbled onto a region progress has passed by and glossed over. I was driving south from Challis on Highway 93 when I crested the Willow Creek Summit. There was a pull-out and I stopped and got out of the car. The sun was setting and its low rays slanted across the wide, grassy valley below. There were a few ranches, and of course the road, insignificant in the vastness, but other than that, nothing to indicate that anyone had ever been to the Lost River Valley before. Walling in the eastern fringe of this basin was a massive, steeply rising mountain range, ragged and streaked with sun rays: the Lost River Range. For me, at that moment, it had the appeal and look of a forgotten world, as if I had just crossed the Himalayas into the secret Tibetan kingdom of the Dalai Lama. Of course it was all fantasy, and I had arrived by car, not yak train. But that first impression of the empty valley and great mountain wall could have given me no greater pleasure than if I had just crossed the Tibetan frontier.

The Lost River is only one range, among a host of others including the Lemhi, White Knobs, Beaverhead, Centennial and Henry's Lake mountains, which lie just north of the Snake River Plain in east-central Idaho. All possess peaks in excess of 10,000', and several ranges like the Lost River and Lemhi exceed 12,000'.

They all have a similar geologic structure in

The upper Pahsimeroi Valley and the Lost River Range. These mountains block what little precipitation arrives from the west, creating a rain-shadow that makes this the driest region in the state. GEORGE WUERTHNER

that they rise abruptly from the surrounding valleys and, for the most part, are long, narrow ranges with broad, open, treeless valleys intervening. These individual mountain blocks were formed when the earth's crust was broken by stretching of the North American Continental Plate as it overrode the Pacific Plate subduction zone. As the earth's crust cracked, mountains were uplifted and the intervening valleys dropped.

All these mountains have some tree cover, however sparse, even though they are very arid. They lie in the rain shadow of high peaks farther west, which wring moisture from the prevailing westerlies. Unlike the mountains of northern Idaho with their mild climate, these ranges experience a sunny, continental climate. Summers are hot and dry; winters are cold and frequently clear. Challis, encircled by mountains, receives only seven inches of precipitation annually.

All these ranges are composed primarily of sedimentary rocks, sometimes overlain by more recent volcanics. Volcanic tuffs, sandstone and limestone are particularly common; water tends to disappear into these rocks and as a result surface run-off is limited. Although sedimentary rocks dominate, a few mountains have small segments of granitic rocks, including the northern Beaverhead and Lemhi ranges.

The lower valleys are dominated by grasslands and once provided forage for herds of bison, bighorn sheep and antelope. These animals supported a low-density, widely scattered Indian population. Prior to the early 1700s and the introduction of the horse, bison were hunted primarily in the winter when hunters on snowshoes could approach the herds confined by deep snows. At other times the hunters might ambush individuals coming to drink at waterholes or passing through narrow canyons.

An infrequently used hunting method involved running an entire herd of bison off a cliff. Near Challis, a historic buffalo jump similar to those on the plains was found by archaeologists in 1971. Although the Indians of this region did kill bison when and where they

At the base of the Lost River Range.
GEORGE WUERTHNER

67

Looking across Henry's Lake to the Henry's Lake Mountains by Targhee Peak. GEORGE WUERTHNER

could, the beast did not constitute their major food source then, because of the limited mobility of Indian people in the pre-horse era. The migratory bison was not always available, and if close by, was dangerous to hunt without the aid of horses. Instead, bighorn sheep or deer, because of their smaller ranges and predictable daily travel routes, were a more dependable source of food. Sheep were hunted by lying in ambush above traditional watering places or hunted with dogs which chased the animals onto the cliffs where hunters could shoot them.

After the arrival of the horse, hunting efficiency increased and bison became a more important food item. Eventually, annual bison hunts were conducted, with some Idaho tribes like the Nez Perce and Shoshone traveling over the mountains and out onto the Montana plains where bison were particularly abundant. Indian trails laced these mountains, and today's roads and highways still follow many of these ancient pathways. The horse caused a dramatic change in Indian social organization. The increase in the food base gave these tribes more

leisure time and enabled them to live in larger groups. Intertribal warfare increased. What the outcome of this social evolution would have been will never be known for, shortly after the arrival of the horse in Idaho, came the white man and the eventual demise of the Indian horse culture.

On August 12, 1805, Meriwether Lewis ascended the Continental Divide in the Beaverhead Mountains and became the first European to enter what would later be known as Idaho. Lewis met a band of Lemhi Shoshone near present-day Tendoy on the Lemhi River. It was a fortuitous meeting because the band's leader was the brother of Sacajawea, the expedition's Shoshone interpreter. The Shoshones sold horses to the travelers, who made an arduous passage through the Bitterroot Mountains to the Clearwater River, which eventually they took to the sea.

Hard on the heels of the Lewis and Clark expedition came the fur trappers searching for beaver pelts. The first trappers were men of the Canadian Northwest Fur Company. One of

these Canadians was Donald MacKenzie, a tireless, 300-pound brigade leader, who as early as 1819 had based his fur hunters in the Little Lost River Valley by present-day Howe. A few years later in 1823, Finnan MacDonald, another Canadian fur brigade leader, and his group of 51 trappers had a battle with Blackfeet Indians along the Lemhi River near Tendoy. MacDonald lost five men before he set fire to the range and burned the Indians out of their entrenchment. Sixty-eight of the Blackfeet were killed. Although MacDonald won the battle, he is quoted as saying "the beaver will have a gould skin" before he would again enter the region. Almost yearly from the 1820s onward, trappers traveled through or skirted these mountains in their quest for fur.

By the 1850s when the first settlers arrived, the beaver were just about gone and many of the trappers became guides and hunters for the new wave of immigrants. One of these immigrant groups was Mormons who, in 1855, built the first permanent settlement in Idaho, just south of present-day Salmon on the Lemhi River. Irrigated farming was begun in the high, dry valley and the settlers named their new mission Limhi after a king in the Book of Mormon. The name, with a slightly different spelling, survived, but the settlement did not. In February of 1858 a group of Bannock Indians (a subgroup of the Shoshone) raided the fort and killed two of the thirty-nine defenders, wounded five others and took off with their cattle. The Mormons withdrew and abandoned their fledgling village.

The next era in settlement did not occur until gold and other mineral discoveries brought miners into the mountains. Since most of this area's mountains are composed of sedimentary rocks, there was less mining activity than elsewhere in the state. Nevertheless, a few mining districts sprang up and communities like Challis and Salmon got their starts as trade centers

for the prospectors. Mackay, in the Lost River Valley, became a supply center around the turn of the century for copper mines in the nearby White Knob Mountains. And Gilmore in the Lemhi Mountains and Nicholia in the Beaverhead Mountains were both established to service people working silver and lead mines.

With the market provided by the miners, the first cattlemen came into the country. It was the open-range era and many parts of these arid mountains were severely overgrazed. Unfortunately, much of this country has never recovered despite nearly a century of range management. Ranching is still the primary industry, but the overall productivity of the land has decreased, making it increasingly difficult for the small family ranches to survive.

Besides ranching, there are some small lumber mills and logging contributes to many local economies. Of all the mountains in this region, the Henry's Lake Mountains have sustained the most logging. These mountains lie west of Yellowstone National Park and form a semicircle along the Continental Divide just north of the Island Park area in what some Idahoans call the "northeast" corner of southern Idaho. The Henry's Lake Mountains are dotted with many open parks and meadows, particularly at higher elevations. The dominant forest cover at lower elevations is lodgepole pine, which has been heavily logged in a belated attempt to salvage pine beetle-infested stands. In the 1960s, the largest single timber sale outside of Alaska, some 318 million board feet, was cut on the Island Park Ranger District of Targhee National Forest for the express purpose of controlling pine beetles. The efforts were largely unsuccessful and the Targhee now has many more clearcuts but not many fewer pine beetles.

If you go high enough in these mountains, you rise above lodgepole stands and enter the subalpine meadows where scattered stands of subalpine fir and limber pine grow. A few of the mountains are even high enough to sustain alpine tundra, including Lionhead Peak (10,080'), Targhee Peak (10,240') and Black Mountain (10,237'). The higher peaks around the Targhee Basin have been glaciated and many cirques, tarns and moraines can be seen.

The limestones and other sedimentary rocks of this range have been thrust up along faults. The area is one of the most active earthquake regions in the western United States. Many tremors and small quakes have been felt in the West Yellowstone-Henry's Lake area, particularly during the last few years. Just on the other side of the Continental Divide in Montana, a major quake in 1959 caused a landslide which buried a campground killing 19 people and blocking the Madison River to form Quake Lake.

The Henry's Lake Mountains are part of the Interagency Grizzly Bear Recovery Team's Situation I grizzly habitat, which is considered essential for the bear's survival. All development here must be conducted so as not to jeopardize the great bear's chances for survival. Besides supporting grizzlies, the area is home to large populations of moose, elk, mule deer and a small herd of 30 bighorn sheep.

West of the Henry's Lake Mountains and grading into one another near Sawtell Peak are the Centennial Mountains, one of the few western mountain ranges with an east-west alignment. This narrow fault block range of uplifted sedimentary limestones and sandstones forms the spine of the Continental Divide between Monida Pass and Red Rock Pass. The range's highest peaks are just under 10,000', with Mt. Jefferson rising to 10,196'. The Montana side of the range is an abrupt fault scarp face with many cliffs and steep terrain. The Idaho side is gentler and rolling in nature. Approximately 80,000 acres on both sides of the range are being studied for possible wilderness designation. Within this proposed wilderness roam several hundred moose, hundreds of elk and an occasional grizzly bear.

Interstate 15 crosses from Idaho into Montana at Monida Pass. The pass is the official break

between the Centennial and the Beaverhead Mountains to the west. The Beaverhead Range runs in a sinuous pattern, first west, then gradually swinging northwest, until it runs into the Bitterroot Mountains near Lost Trail Pass by Salmon. (Some people consider the Beaverhead as merely a southern extension of the Bitterroot Range.) On the western face of the mountains, particularly in the Lemhi River valley, the steep, high face of the mountains with their heavily glaciated peaks is an impressive sight. Some of the high peaks include Red Conglomerate (10,106'), Italian Peak (10,998'), Scott Peak (11,393'), Webber Peak (11,223') and other equally high summits. The Continental Divide runs the entire length of the range, separating Montana from Idaho.

An interesting bit of history is reflected near Lost Trail Pass just north of the Beaverhead Mountains. The Continental Divide was supposed to form the border between the two states all the way from Yellowstone Park to the Canadian border. Yet, here, if you check a map you'll note that the Continental Divide curves northeast along the Anaconda-Pintler Mountains in Montana, while the border of Idaho and Montana swings west and then northward following the Bitterroot Divide. The reason for the discrepancy can be attributed to maneuvers in the U.S. Congress. Sidney Edgerton, chief justice of Idaho Territory, led the fight for splitting off Montana at the Continental Divide. Idaho's legislature had agreed that the original territory was too large, and the Rockies made a significant barrier in its middle. But Idaho's legislators were unpleasantly surprised when Edgerton, in Washington, D.C., added three degrees of longitude to Montana Territory's western edge. The border would run down the crest of the Bitterroots, leaving the narrow Idaho panhandle. The Flathead and Kootenai valleys became part of Montana Territory, whose first governor was none other than Edgerton.

A ranch below the 10,000' peaks of the Beaverhead Range near the town of Salmon. GEORGE WUERTHNER

In the not-too-distant geological past, the Beaverhead Mountains actually were west of the divide. Instead of flowing west, the Salmon River flowed across what are now the Beaverhead Mountains to the Missouri River drainage and eventually into Hudson's Bay. It was only in comparatively recent geologic time that the Salmon River waters were captured by a stream flowing from the west and the river took on its present course.

The sedimentary limestones and sandstones that prevail in the southern portion of the Beaverheads have little surface drainage and few lakes. As a result, much of the range is covered with grass and sage with high grassy divides and extensive rolling alpine meadows where alpine glaciation did not sharpen the ridges. Forests of Douglas fir, lodgepole pine, aspen, subalpine fir, Englemann spruce and limber pine are usually found only in scattered patches, primarily on the north slopes and in bowls and hollows. Alpine tundra exists on the highest slopes and peaks.

On these higher slopes one may see the mountain goat, which reaches its natural southern limits in this portion of the state. Goats found farther south in Idaho and in other states like Colorado are all the result of transplants. In the Beaverhead goats are found in the Red Conglomerate Peaks, Italian Peaks and farther north by Salmon. In a pattern that has occurred all too frequently in the west, increased hunter road access followed the logging of higher basins near Salmon during the 1970s. The result was a severe decline of goat populations and all goat hunting in this part of the range was terminated in the 1980s.

Another mammal that reaches its southern limits in these mountains near Freeman Peak is the hoary marmot, a groundhog-like rodent that inhabits high, alpine areas from Alaska south to the Beaverhead. In addition to these alpine animals, one of the largest antelope herds in Idaho roams the valleys and highlands along Birch and Medicine Lodge creeks. Approximately 2,000 animals are estimated to live at least part of the year in the lower valleys of these mountains. On ground higher than the antelope prefers, one might see the 50 bighorn sheep known to inhabit the Webber Creek area by Italian Peak. In 1984, 25 additional sheep were transplanted to Hawley Creek on the Salmon National Forest and more transplants are planned for the near future.

Mule deer are extremely plentiful, and an estimated 5,000 deer live on the northern part of the Beaverhead Mountains. In addition,

71

Sunrise on the Lemhi Range near Bell Mountain, as seen from Birch Creek Valley. The Lemhis form the longest range (100 miles) in the state without a road crossing.
GEORGE WUERTHNER

some 1,500 elk summer over the range in Montana's Big Hole Valley and then cross the mountains to winter in Idaho. Moose are scattered throughout the range, but are not common. Even a few grizzlies may roam the mountains: a grizzly was sighted in the Italian Peaks area a few years ago, an area significantly west of its normal range near Yellowstone National Park. As may be expected, these game-rich mountains attract many hunters from throughout the state and hunting is important to the local economy in the autumn after the tourist season.

Today's hunters are merely following in the footsteps of many others who came before them. In rock recesses along Birch Creek are several important archaeological sites, including Jaguar Cave a few miles north of Lone Pine, where a hearth yielded a radiocarbon date of 11,580 years. Inside this rock shelter, researchers

have collected the remains of camel, collared lemming, dire wolf and lion as well as 40 other species.

In an effort to keep these areas looking as they did when the first primitive hunters entered this part of Idaho, conservationists have proposed several wilderness areas along the length of the Beaverhead Mountains: in the Garfield-Red Conglomerate Peaks is a 90,000-acre roadless area, another 318,000 acres from Scott Peak north to Eighteenmile Peak is also roadless, and approximately 100,000 acres just east of Salmon are part of the West Big Hole proposed wilderness. These lands are some of the more remote and important big game habitat in the state and certainly deserve wilderness classification.

Should you stand on the crest of the Beaverhead Mountains and look west, you will be

peering at the longest unbroken mountain mass in Idaho—the 100-mile-long Lemhi Range. It is flanked on the west by the Pahsimeroi and Little Lost River valleys and on the east by Birch Creek and the Lemhi River. The highest peak, Diamond (12,197') is one of the few in the state that rises above 12,000' and scores of other peaks are 10,000' to 11,000' in elevation. Over 500,000 acres of the Lemhis are roadless, making this one of the largest undesignated roadless areas in the state—some groups have proposed that the entire range be given wilderness classification.

Cirques, glacial erratics, moraines and hanging valleys can all be found. The southern portion of the range is predominantly limestone formed under ancient seas, but to the north are less permeable quartzites and some younger mineral intrusions, including outcrops of granitic

The Lost River Range is so little explored that, of nine peaks over 12,000' in elevation, only three are named. GEORGE WUERTHNER

rock. Along the contact point between the granites and sedimentary rocks, mineralization occurs; several silver-lead deposits were mined, including one in a large mine where the town of Gilmore once existed.

Although the Lemhi Range is in the rain shadow of higher mountains to the west, its western slope is better watered than the eastern, and there is greater surface run-off, and more cirque lakes in the quartzites of the north than on the limestones of the south. As a result, wildlife is more abundant in the western and northern portions, with some 1,000 elk, 2,000 or so mule deer, 170 mountain goats and a few black bears rounding out the big game species. As in the nearby Beaverhead, mountain goat populations were severely depleted by over-hunting; the season was closed in 1974 and has not yet reopened.

West of the Lemhi is the Lost River Range, which has Idaho's highest mountains. The range is sometimes further broken down into three sub-ranges beginning with the Pahsimeroi in the north, which runs from Challis south to Double Spring Pass. The central section containing Mt. Borah (Idaho's tallest peak) is usually considered the Lost River Range proper and south of Pass Creek the range is sometimes referred to as the King Mountain area. Geologically, there are no distinctions; it is all one upthrusted block of limestone and I prefer to call the entire unit the Lost River Range.

The Lost River Range could be considered Idaho's rooftop, for nine of the eleven peaks over 12,000' in elevation are found here. Of these nine, only three have names: Borah at 12,662', Leatherman (12,288') and Breitenbach

(12,140'). Unlike in the California Sierra and other heavily traveled mountains where it seems almost every boulder has a name, the Lost River Range is little visited, hence there are dozens of unnamed peaks of 10,000' and 11,000' in elevation.

As might be expected, the great heights of these peaks harbored glaciers which carved sharp aretes, cirque basins and U-shaped canyons. As in most limestone ranges, there are few lakes since water tends to sink into the permeable rock.

The past glaciation along with the Lost Rivers' steep western flank presents a dramatic face to travelers driving Highway 93 between Arco and Challis. The peaks rise 5,000' above the Big Lost River Valley and may still be rising higher. On October 28, 1983 a large earthquake measuring 7.3 on the Richter scale shook

73

Mount Borah (12,662' prior to the 1983 earthquake) is Idaho's highest mountain. GEORGE WUERTHNER

the Rockies. The quake's epicenter was along the base of Mt. Borah and a fault scar ten miles long now adorns the west slope of the range where the valley dropped between 15' and 20'. I was living some 300 miles distant from the epicenter, in Bozeman, Montana. During breakfast, the entire house shook, swaying plants and rattling dishes. I was still half asleep and my first thought was that a freight train must be passing close by—then I remembered there were not tracks within miles of my house. It was only then I realized that an earthquake was occurring. This was the largest quake to shake the lower 48 states in 24 years!

Mt. Borah is named for William Borah, a lawyer and Republican Senator from Idaho between 1907 and 1940. Borah never climbed his namesake, but almost anyone in reasonably good health can make the summit. There is one narrow ridge where dropoffs of several thousand feet might make some people uncomfortable, but the entire climb is considered non-technical. Water is a problem if you climb late in the year, since the snow melts off early from the windswept, barren peak. I once began the climb late one evening and spent the night near the top expecting to find a stream or spring to replenish my water supply. There was none. Suffering from thirst, I nevertheless pushed on to the summit and found the expansive view of the Lost River Valley below and the ragged edge of the distant Boulder, White Cloud and Sawtooth mountains, seen in the early morning light, easily worth the dehydration incurred.

The Lost Rivers are so high and so arid, they have a double timberline: a lower one because of a lack of moisture and an upper one because of cold. Growing on the slopes are Douglas fir, mountain mahogany, juniper and limber pine. Primarily because of overgrazing, sagebrush now dominates many of the lower slopes where grass used to be abundant.

With their overall steep terrain, lack of wa-

The White Knob Mountains, viewed across the East Fork of the Big Lost River, are the virtually unknown site of several 11,000' peaks. GEORGE WUERTHNER

ter and lack of escape cover, the Lost River never did sustain a large big-game population. Approximately 1,000 elk, all descendants of transplants, roam the mountains. Bighorn sheep, once more numerous than deer in this area, were exterminated by the turn of the century; replanted, they now number 250 individuals. Apparently the Lost River were too arid for goats, for none ever existed here. Moose are also notably absent.

If the Lost River Range can be considered relatively unknown by most state residents and outsiders, then the nearby White Knob Mountains, which lie west of Mackay, are *terra incognita*. These high, rolling limestone and volcanic peaks exceed 11,000' in elevation, mak-

ing them one of the higher mountain masses in the state, yet most people would be hard-pressed to recognize their name, much less locate them on a map. Still, there are peaks like Shelly Mountain (11,278'), Lime Mountain (11,179'), Mackay Peak (10,273') and Porphyry Peak (10,012'), which are among the 50 highest peaks in the state.

That the White Knob are known at all is probably the result of intrusions that included copper. This attracted the attention of George Mackay, who built a railroad from Blackfoot to the White Knob Mountains to service the mines. A townsite was laid out below the mine and a smelter was built. But the mines failed and closed. Nevertheless, the town of Mackay

remained as a service center for nearby ranches and other outlying mining ventures.

The Broad Valley ranges are some of Idaho's most majestic mountains, and of all the high places in the state, my personal favorites. There is a clarity of light, a vastness that is sweeping yet contained by distant peaks, which makes such distances comprehensible. To me the name Lost River has a significance that goes beyond just its role as a place on the maps: This region is an anachronism in a world of vacation ranchettes and real estate developments. No doubt these will come in time, but for now these Broad Valley ranges are just a bit too raw-edged and harsh to suit most people's taste. That, in itself, is their best protection.

10

SOUTHEAST IDAHO

Hoarfrost covers sagebrush in the Bear River Valley south of Soda Springs. In the background are the low, rounded peaks of the Bear River Range. GEORGE WUERTHNER

THE OVERTHRUST BELT

The mountains of southeastern Idaho, with few exceptions, are not as rugged or as majestic as those in other parts of the state. You won't see jagged peaks like the Sawtooth, or steep, timbered valleys as in the Clearwater—at least not many. But this less steep, less rugged terrain has its own appeal. Rather than repelling exploration, the gentleness is inviting; the open forests of aspen, fir and pine, the spacious meadows and grassy knolls make for sweeping vistas and a vegetation mosaic that, like dabbled light in a forest glade, offers many shades and textures of green.

Determining where one range ends and the next begins is not always easy, and there often are several names for the same range of mountains. For example, the mountains to the west of Bear Lake are called the Bear River Range or the Wasatch Range depending upon which map you consult. In other places a long ridge of mountains might appear on maps as several subranges such as the Bannock Range, which extends from Pocatello south into Utah and is sometimes further divided into the Elkhorn Range, Oxford Peak Range and, once it enters Utah, the Wellsville Mountains.

For all their ambiguity of names, these ranges have a very similar geological history and consist primarily of sedimentary or metamorphic deposits laid down when this region was the western margin of the North American plate; in nearly all these ranges shales, limestones, quartzite and sandstones predominate. The ancient ocean deposits were broken and the rock strata pushed 30 to 40 miles eastward, so that older strata now cover younger rocks in a great structure caused by crustal movement known as the Overthrust Belt. In other parts of the Overthrust Belt petroleum has been discovered, so the Idaho ranges of the Over-

Aspen groves in Booth Canyon along Palisades Reservoir in the Snake River Range. JEFF GNASS

thrust are now actively being explored for oil and gas.

These mountains are not as arid as those of the Basin and Range province, but nevertheless annual precipitation is still much lower than that of northern Idaho. The climate is moist enough to support trees on many of the higher mountains; however, grasses, sage and other shrubs still dominate the lower slopes and drier areas.

Compared to other regions of the state, these mountains, particularly the Caribou, Aspen, Snake River Range and others near the Wyoming border, have a large proportion of aspen and lodgepole pine. Both species require a great deal of sunlight for successful seed germination and seedling growth, and are known as fire-adapted species.

For example, lodgepole pine, a quick-growing, early-maturing species that invades disturbed areas, will often completely dominate a site for a hundred years or so. But young lodgepole pine cannot grow and survive in the shade of dense canopies, including those created by their own parents. Eventually, if nothing intervenes, the pine forest will be replaced by other species such as subalpine fir, which is very shade-tolerant and can grow in the understory of a forest. Before the white man began to suppress fires around the turn of the century, lodgepole pine forests burned frequently, which created the ideal conditions of bare mineral soil and lots of sunlight so necessary for its seeds to germinate and survive. In many areas the cones of lodgepole pine will not even open unless heated, further tying it to a dependence upon fires for successful regeneration.

If, for some reason, a fire fails to burn an area for 80 to 100 years, other species such as fir begin to dominate the site. At this point, lodgepole reaches an age and size that make it susceptible to pine beetle infestations. The beetles seldom attack young pines, only those reaching, or past, their primes. If the pine beetle epidemic is successful, many lodgepoles will die, creating a high fuel loading, ready to ignite. Even if the site does not burn, the pine beetle may kill enough lodgepoles to open the canopy so that young pines can establish themselves. In essence, lodgepole pines use the pine beetle to help thin the forest and keep it healthy.

Aspen, another fire-dependent species, is found in all southeastern Idaho ranges. Some ranges, like the Caribou, Bear River and Aspen, are covered with aspen groves. Although these groves appear to be healthy, a closer look reveals that there are very few young groves and nearly all existing groves are past their prime and dying. Increasing shade from a closing canopy, competition from conifers and, in some cases, overbrowsing by livestock and wildlife have drastically reduced the number of aspen saplings. Some scientists speculate that unless the trend is reversed, aspen groves will gradually die out and disappear from these mountains.

In the arid west, aspens seldom successfully reproduce by seed. Instead, nearly all existing groves have regenerated themselves from existing root systems by a means called suckering. When the adult aspen is toppled, whether by fire, a beaver or the ax of man, hormones stimulate growth of root nodes that grow upwards and become new saplings. But these saplings will survive only if they have plenty of light, water and nutrients—the kind of conditions that exist after a fire. In the past, fires provided the stimuli needed to boost aspen sucker production, but today few wildfires are allowed to burn and many groves are being over-

Wheatfield in the Cache Valley. STEPHEN TRIMBLE

taken by the more shade-tolerant fir and spruce.

It was partly the abundance of aspen that fueled the explorations of the first Europeans to enter southeastern Idaho's mountains, for aspen is a favorite food of beaver, and the pursuit of beaver pelts spawned the Rocky Mountain fur trade. The mountain men, as the fur trappers were called, found a wildlife assortment and abundance in southeastern Idaho surpassed only by the game-rich plains of Montana. Buffalo, grizzly, wolves and bighorn sheep were all common. None of these species exists here today. Other species such as mule deer, elk, moose, black bear, marten, beaver and mountain

lion survived the guns, traps and poisons of the stockmen and market hunters and are still found in the region. Interestingly, archaeological evidence shows that, prior to the introduction of the horse, Indians killed more mountain sheep than any other big game animal, including bison, probably because sheep tend to use the same ranges year around and they make relatively predictable movements. The unmounted Indians could not effectively exploit migratory animals like the bison except under special circumstances.

The first trapper to enter this part of Idaho was John Colter, a former member of the Lewis and Clark party. In 1808 Colter traveled over Teton Pass into the Teton Valley near present-day Driggs. Shortly thereafter, other trappers and explorers followed. Within a few years, southeastern Idaho was becoming crowded as rival fur companies converged on the region to trap and hunt in this wildlife-rich area.

By the 1820s many whose names became famous in the annals of the fur trade were ranging widely through these mountains and valleys, including Jedediah Smith, Alexander Ross, Jim Bridger, Donald MacKenzie, John Weber, Peter Skene Ogden. Their names are now attached to places throughout the west. The Weber River in Utah, Ross' Hole in Montana, the Jedediah Smith Wilderness and Bridger National Forest in Wyoming—all bear the names of these early frontiersmen. One can only guess at the impact they had on the wildlife; Ogden gives us a clue when he reports that his men collected 2,440 beaver pelts from southeastern Idaho in one season.

Unlike our cultural image of the trapper as a lone individual living a hermit life in the high fastness of the Rockies, most mountain men traveled in large groups, called fur brigades, to discourage Indian attacks. Many of these men loved the life in the mountains and had little desire to make a yearly arduous journey back to the settlements for trade goods, so a new system was developed. Goods were brought west to a prearranged meeting ground or rendezvous where the trappers could sell their furs, obtain their yearly supply of traps, blankets, powder, shot, knives and trinkets, and engage in a general melee of horseracing, gambling and drunken brawls. All in all, good, wholesome all-American fun.

The abundance and diversity of wildlife in southeastern Idaho can only be appreciated by reading the journals of these early trappers and explorers, and one gets the impression that this part of Idaho was once an American Serengeti. For example, passing through the Portneuf, Bear River and Salt River valleys in 1832, Nathaniel Wyeth reported seeing large numbers of antelope, buffalo, grizzlies and mountain sheep. The naturalist John Townsend, describing the area near the Portneuf River in 1834, wrote, "Our present camp is a beautiful one. A rich and open plain of luxuriant grass, dotted with buffalo in all directions, a high picturesque hill in front, and a lovely stream of cold mountain water flowing at our feet... This evening the roaring of the bulls in the gang near us is terrific, and these sounds are mingled with the howling of large packs of wolves, which regularly attend upon them, and the hoarse screaming of hundreds of ravens flying overhead. The dreaded grizzly bear is also quite common in this neighborhood; two have been seen in some bushes near by, and they visit our camp almost every night, attracted by the piles of meat which are heaped all around." Despite this abundance in 1832, by 1845 bison were difficult to find in Idaho and by 1860 they were extinct in the state.

The fur trade was essentially dead by the 1840s because of the virtual extinction of the beaver and changes in European fashions that stopped the demand for beaver pelts.

Idaho's first town, Franklin, in the Cache Valley by the Bear River Range, was established by Mormons in 1860. The Mormons showed that irrigation with water from the surrounding mountains could sustain agriculture in Idaho, and soon other Mormon settlements followed, including Soda Springs in 1862, Paris in 1863 and Montpelier in 1864. Many of these communities grazed cattle and sheep in the

Beaver dam in the Bannock Mountains. Aspen cut by beavers likely resprouts, providing new food.
GEORGE WUERTHNER

79

Slope of Mt. Bonneville looking toward Haystack Mountain in the Portneuf Range near Pocatello.
GEORGE WUERTHNER

nearby mountains and gradually individuals started ranches in the more isolated mountain valleys. By 1900 unrestricted grazing of mountain pastures resulted in overgrazing and consequent erosion of mountain soils. Gradual reductions in the numbers of livestock grazing the public lands have led to some improvement, but the sad fact is that a greater percentage of rangelands is in poor ecological condition than is healthy and productive.

In the 1860s and '70s miners began to roam southeastern Idaho seeking gold and silver deposits, only to be foiled by the generally unmineralized sedimentary rocks. The only major gold rush here occurred in the Caribou Range in 1870.

Unlike in other parts of Idaho, logging did not replace mining as a major economic force. In these southeast mountains trees grow slowly and stands are frequently scattered, thus discouraging commercial logging. Timber har-

vesting, although common, is only marginally profitable and has never been as important here as in other parts of the state.

Seeing the Bannock Range just west of Pocatello for the first time, one may wonder how any timber industry could occur. This 100-mile-long, north-south-trending range seems to be covered with hardly any vegetation at all; what little there is seems to be mostly sagebrush, rabbitbrush, bitterbrush and an occasional juniper. At least this is the impression one would get as you drive by the range on Interstate 15. Actually, like many of these southeastern Idaho ranges, the Bannock Range has a good forest cover of aspen and old-growth Douglas fir, once you gain enough elevation.

Elevational gain there is aplenty: nearly 4,500' of relief between the Cache Valley and some of the higher peaks like Oxford (9,281') and Elkhorn (9,001'). But unlike mountains elsewhere in Idaho where glaciation has been

extensive, the Bannock Range's gentle features mask its actual height and make it appear less dramatic. Evidence of the Ice Age is nevertheless visible as terraces between 4,800' and 5,200' on the slopes of the Bannock Range, where the ancient shorelines of glacial Lake Bonneville once reached. At Red Rock Pass at the north end of Cache Valley, Lake Bonneville once had an outlet down Marsh Creek and the Portneuf River into the Snake River. Apparently the lake cut its outlet rapidly, for there is evidence of one or more huge floods. Giant scour marks and water-rounded boulders are common on the old flood route along Marsh Creek.

Cache Valley got its name from early trappers who left a deposit of furs here during the mountain-man era. The valley was a favorite haunt of both Indian and whites and the trapper Osborn Russell notes in his journal that there were "large quantities of beaver and otter" in the valley and nearby mountains.

Across the Cache and Marsh Creek valleys from the Bannock Range is the Portneuf Range, named for a member of Peter Skene Ogden's trapping party who was killed here by Indians in 1825. Like the Bannock Range, the Portneuf is of gentle and rolling relief with a number of low passes separating higher summits. The highest peak is Mt. Bonneville, which at 9,260' is just high enough to have been glaciated. Other high peaks include Haystack Mountain (9,025') and Sedgwick Peak (9,167'). The Portneuf Range is a continuation of the Overthrust Belt, and like the Bannock Range, also consists primarily of quartzites, siltstones and limestones.

The entire Portneuf Range is grazed by domestic livestock as are most of the southeastern Idaho ranges. These domestic animals share the ranges with mule deer and an occasional elk. A small population of 10 to 15 moose is found here and is thought to be expanding its distribution and numbers.

To the south of the Portneuf Range across Oneida Narrows is the northward extension of Utah's Wasatch Range, referred to locally as the Bear River Range. The Oneida Narrows canyon was carved by the Bear River when its former northward course to the Snake River was blocked by lava flows in the Gem Valley. It is here, near the mouth of this canyon at Battle Creek, that one of the single greatest Indian losses in the west took place in January 1863, when a group of California volunteers led by P.E. Conner surprised a winter encampment of Shoshone Indians, killing 400. More Indians died here than at the Little Bighorn, Sand Creek and other more famous Indian battles.

The Bear River Range itself is a horst block between the Gem Valley graben and Bear Lake graben. (A graben is a valley which is bounded on its sides by upthrusted faults called horsts. The valley itself drops.) The range rises some 4,000' above the surrounding valleys, with Sherman Peak at 9,669' and Paris Peak at 9,587' as the highest summits. Some of the higher peaks were glaciated. Bloomington Lakes near the crest of the mountains occupy glacial cirques.

The core of the range is underlain by limestone and there are few surface streams, since most of the water sinks into the limestone to emerge as large springs in Cub, St. Charles and Paris Canyons. Caves are common, and Minnetonka Cave in St. Charles Canyon is the largest commercially developed cave in Idaho. One of its rooms, called the "Ballroom," is 90' high and more than 300' across.

The Bear River Range extends across the state border into Utah and this portion of the range has been designated the Mt. Naomi Wilderness as part of the 1984 Utah Wilderness Bill. Idaho conservationists are proposing that some 64,000 acres along the crest of the Bear River Range in Idaho be added to the wilderness system. Wilderness designation would help to preserve the lush beauty of the mountain meadows along the range's crest.

The Bear River Range is cloaked in aspen intermixed with a Great Basin species, bigtooth maple, a close kin of the sugar maple common in the east, which reaches the northernmost limits of its range here. The maple turns a brilliant red in the fall, and along with the golden yellows of aspen, makes for unforgettable autumn colors.

North of Bear River to the east of Georgetown

Caribou Mountain as seen across Gray's Lake Wildlife Refuge. The Caribous are a series of ridges separated by narrow, shallow valleys. JEFF GNASS

and Soda Springs are a number of low, narrow, parallel ridges, separated by valleys one to three miles across, comprising the Aspen, Preuss, Gray's Lake, Webster and other hilly ridges. Meade Peak at 9,953' is the highest eminence among these rolling ranges. The low ridges, separated by narrow valleys, are manifestations of the Overthrust faulting in which older rock strata were pushed over young rock layers. Nearly all these ranges consist of sedimentary limestones, sandstones and siltstones, which formed along the edge of the Continental margin in shallow seas. One formation, the Phosphora, is mined as phosphate at Soda Springs and Georgetown.

Located in a high mountain valley at the northern end of the Gray's Lake Range is Gray's Lake. The lake is actually a marshy swamp and part of the Gray's Lake Wildlife Refuge. The lake name was misspelled from that of John Grey, a part-Iroquois trapper who explored the area in 1818 as part of a Canadian

fur brigade. The refuge produces about 5,000 ducks and 2,000 geese each year and the nesting colony of Franklin's gulls sometimes numbers 40,000 individuals.

One of the rarest animals seen at the refuge is the whooping crane. The naturalist John Townsend, who passed through the Soda Springs area in 1834, found whooping cranes and white pelicans abundant. But by 1941 only 21 five-feet-tall cranes remained in the wild because of habitat destruction and over-hunting; by 1948 only 15 wild birds remained. Today the population consists of both wild and captive birds and still numbers no more than 60.

Each year the cranes complete a hazardous 2,500-mile migration between their wintering grounds on the Texas coast and their breeding area in the remote marshes of Wood Buffalo National Park in Canada. During the nesting season, the female lays two eggs but only one hatches. Since 1967, the extra eggs from each nest have been artificially incubated at the Pa-

High peaks of the Snake Range (also called Palisades). GEORGE WUERTHNER

Caribou Mountain as seen from the Caribou Basin. GEORGE WUERTHNER

tuxent Wildlife Research Center in Maryland. In 1975 the Fish and Wildlife Service began to use the more common, but smaller, sandhill cranes that nest at Gray's Lake as foster parents for eggs produced by wild and captive whoopers. The sandhills readily adopt the young whoopers and teach them how to survive in the wild. Today some of the adopted whooping cranes migrate with the sandhills between their wintering grounds and Gray's Lake. It is hoped that, eventually, a second flock of whooping cranes will establish themselves in the west, and help to ensure survival of this majestic white bird.

Rising beyond Gray's Lake is 9,803' Caribou Mountain, the second highest peak in southeastern Idaho and an igneous intrusion within the otherwise sedimentary Caribou Range. Glaciers once clad Caribou Mountain's flanks, as well as those of nearby Big Elk Mountain, steepening the slopes and carving out cirques,

but most of the range exhibits the gentle, rolling terrain so characteristic of many mountains in this region. Caribou Peak was the site of a major gold rush in 1870, when placer deposits were discovered on McCoy Creek by Jesse "Caribou Jack" Fairchild. The mining era lasted 20 years and eventually some $50 million worth of gold were washed out of nearby streams. The towns of Kennan (pop. 500) and Caribou (pop. 1,500) were established and, as in many Idaho gold rush communities, more than half the miners were Chinese. Today these settlements are ghost towns.

Along the eastern edge of the Caribou Range are large salt beds, from which the nearby Salt River gets its name. Along Crow, Tygee and Stump creeks there are salt springs. The area attracted Indians, trappers and even travelers on the Oregon Trail, who all came to gather the salt crystallized on the ground surrounding the springs.

Although most of the Caribou Range has been leased for oil and gas exploration, conservationists have proposed that 200,000 acres in two units be designated as wilderness.

Across the South Fork of the Snake River, beyond Palisades Reservoir, is a northwest-southeast-trending mountain chain referred to as the Big Hole Mountains, Snake River Range (Palisades), or the Salt Range after it enters Wyoming. The entire chain is geologically related and consists of limestones, shales and sandstones that, like rocks of other ranges in this part of Idaho, have been thrust faulted on edge. But unlike most other southeastern Idaho mountains, these ranges have been heavily glaciated, particularly near the Wyoming-Idaho border. The most northerly end of the range, often called the Big Hole Mountains, lies north of Pine Creek Pass. The highest peaks include 9,019' Piney Creek and 9,016' Garns Mountain. South of Pine Creek Pass, one enters the main Snake River Range with 10,025' Mt. Baird among the higher peaks. The Snake River Range rises quite abruptly from the South Fork of the Snake River valley and has some very steep terrain. Although forest cover is nearly continuous, there are many meadows, sage-covered slopes and other natural openings.

These mountains are the heart of the Idaho Overthrust Belt and are under heavy pressure for oil and gas exploration. At the same time, these ranges are valued for their wildlife and recreational values and are under consideration for wilderness designation. The significance of this area for wildlands preservation is apparent by the designation of the Wyoming portion of the Snake River Range as a wilderness study area in the 1984 Wyoming Wilderness Bill. Within the Idaho portion of the Snake River Range is the 111,000-acre proposed Palisades Wilderness and the 78,000-acre Garns Mountain proposed wilderness in the Big Hole.

Just north of the Snake River Range lies the large mountain valley (30 miles long and 15 miles wide) known as Pierre's Hole. A "hole" was the name given by the mountain men to any mountain-rimmed high valley. Scattered across the Rockies are other such-named valleys: Jackson Hole in Wyoming, Brown's Hole in Colorado, the Big Hole in Montana. John Colter was the first white man to see Pierre's Hole when, in 1808, he crossed Teton Pass from Wyoming alone during a winter scouting trip. Seventeen years later, in 1835, Osborn Russell entered Pierre's Hole and found a "beautiful valley consisting of a smooth plain intersected by small streams and thickly clothed with grass and herbage and abounds with buffaloe, elk, deer and antelope etc."

These mountains surrounding Pierre's Hole are home to elk, mule deer, moose, mountain lion, pika, yellow-bellied marmot and are the southern range limits of the great gray owl. Some 1,500 elk winter in the Palisades south of the valley and another 500 in the Big Hole to the west. Mountain goats were transplanted to the Snake River Range (Palisades) 15 years ago and now number between 120 and 150. They

Sunset in the Swan Valley below the Big Hole Mountains. JEFF GNASS

have recently been sighted north of Teton Pass in Grand Teton National Park, which poses a philosophical problem for the Park Service policy of maintaining natural ecosystems. The goats are not native to the region and may well harm the plant life and they compete with a small remnant herd of 120 bighorn sheep that roam the western slope of the Tetons.

In the foothills of the Tetons on the eastern border of Pierre's Hole, grizzly bears are occasionally seen, particularly in Convent and Boone creeks. The Tetons themselves are not actually in Idaho, though the peaks form a spectacular backdrop to the town of Driggs and many Idahoans, no doubt, consider these moun-

tains as part of their state.

Southeastern Idaho is one of the state's forgotten mountain areas, which people automatically assume to have no unique beauty because they lack special designations like wilderness or national recreation area status, but it would be a mistake to write off such a naturally alluring and inviting part of the state. Here is a comfortable balance between spacious valleys and rolling peaks, a place where you can get out and walk around without having to be half mountain goat and half grizzly, or need a machete to clear a passage through the dense brush. Here then, is a mountain terrain of human dimensions.

11

BASIN AND RANGE

The Albion Range in southern Idaho boasts 10,000' peaks. GEORGE WUERTHNER

As you drive north from Salt Lake City toward Boise along Interstate 84, you cross into Idaho near the town of Snowville, Utah, and without fanfare you have also entered into the northwestern fringe of the Basin and Range province. In this part of Idaho there are fairly high, prominent mountains scattered across the landscape, with wide intervening valleys. If you pay attention to mountains at all, you probably silently note that these peaks are quite high, at least look high, and you're taken by surprise. "What are high mountains doing out here where I don't expect mountains?" You might even, as I did, glance at a map to see how high these peaks really are. Ten thousand feet! Yes, a few peaks do exceed 10,000' and quite a few more are a respectable 9,000'-plus. But unless you live in Twin Falls or Burley or someplace else close by, you probably never heard of a single range: the Cassia, Albion, Sublette, Black Pine and Deep Creek mountains. Yet there they rest, sweeping across the horizon, unmistakably good-sized mountains, not hills. And if you are exceptionally curious, as I was, you forget about racing home and take the exit off the freeway and head toward those high peaks to see what Idaho's Basin and Range mountains really look like up close.

These mountains are the northern outliers of a geographical province that covers most of Nevada, western Utah and parts of Arizona, California and, of course, southern Idaho. Geographers characterize the Basin and Range as typically fault block mountains with large, intervening valleys—the basins referred to in their name. For the most part, the Basin and Range mountains have no external drainage; rivers cascade down out of the peaks, then slowly sink out of sight in the hot, dry valleys before they pass out of the region. But the *Idaho* Basin and Range mountains are an exception and several creeks and very small rivers do drain

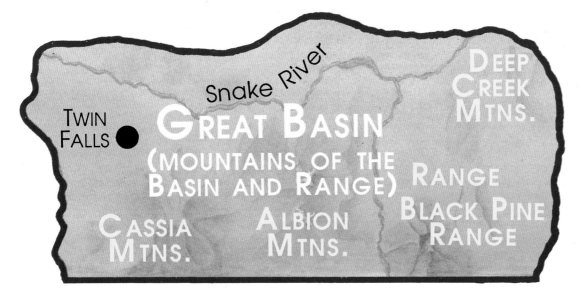

Juniper-pinyon pine forests on the lower slopes of the Albion Range. GEORGE WUERTHNER

Aspen in the Sublette Range. STEPHEN TRIMBLE

north to the Snake River and eventually leave the state.

If you couldn't tell while racing north along the freeway, it becomes immediately apparent once you get close to any of these ranges, that they are arid. Not just a bit underwatered, but dry. At the lowest elevations, where over-grazing has not been too serious, there are rich grasslands and of course the ubiquitous sage-brush. The slopes have a gray-green color from the prevalence of sage. Then, at around 7,000' elevation a curious dark band of vegetation, visible from a distance, rings many of the mountains. Above this band, grasslands domi-nate, sometimes all the way to timberline. No trees beyond this point, at least not on many south slopes. The dark band represents the most northward extension of the juniper-pinyon for-est which is very common over broad areas of Arizona, Utah, Nevada and eastern Califor-nia. Climb around the backside of these peaks and you will find other trees like aspen, Douglas fir and lodgepole pine, but usually on the moister, north slopes. From the south, except for the juniper-pinyon, these mountains appear barren of trees.

The lack of trees is very likely one reason you, in all likelihood, had never heard of the Al-bion Range or the Black Pine Range. There is little, if any, logging in these mountains. On top of that the geological structure consists of sedi-mentary rocks which usually have limited mineral potential and these mountains are no exception. Mining occurred, but there were no big strikes that brought thousands of gold seekers pouring into these hills. And while the mountains are big and brawny, they are not rugged and filled with cool, blue lakes like the Sawtooth or the peaks of north Idaho, so that recreation use, except by locals, has thus far remained rather limited. Livestock grazing has been, and continues to be, the major land use in all of these ranges. Basically, from the usual human perspective, these mountains are pretty useless. Not much in them to exploit and hence you won't read about them in history books, geology books or even tourist promotion litera-ture. This is Idaho's weedpatch, the back forty left to fallow. But if you are a mountain lover, these are beautiful ranges, friendly, welcoming and alluring.

The most westerly of these ranges is the Cassia Mountain Range. People in Twin Falls call them the South Hills, and indeed, if you

are in Twin Falls looking south, these low, plateau-like mountains do seem more like hills than mountains. The higher peaks barely nudge 8,000', with Monument Peak, at 8,060', the high-est. The core of the range consists of limestones and siltstones, but these are often covered by much younger volcanic ash and tuffs.

Because of their relative isolation from other mountains, the Cassia have fewer than a half dozen tree species. Aspen is the most abundant species and relatively common throughout the range. Lodgepole pine occupies the mid forest zones, with subalpine fir as the timberline spe-cies. Douglas fir occurs, but it is rare.

As in all these Idaho Basin and Range moun-tains, grizzly bears once roamed the Cassia, but were exterminated when the livestock industry arrived in the late 1800s. Bighorn sheep were also common, but miners and market hunters eliminated them by the turn of the century. The Idaho Fish and Game Department plans to reintroduce bighorns from the Owyhee Moun-tains into the Cassia within the next year or two. But it is doubtful if they will ever bring back the grizzly. Mule deer are quite abundant, yet there are no elk in this range. Since a number of the creeks in the Cassia flow into the

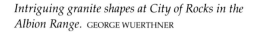

Intriguing granite shapes at City of Rocks in the Albion Range. GEORGE WUERTHNER

names like Elephant Rock, Dragon's Head and Giant Toadstool. The grassy valley fringed by pinyon pine, juniper and aspen was a favorite campsite for California-bound immigrants traveling the Oregon Trail during the mid-1800s. Like many unusual rock formations and mountains in the west, the City of Rocks has its own version of a buried treasure tale. In 1878 an overland stage express was robbed of a cargo worth $90,000. The bandits were eventually captured. One was killed and the other died in jail, but only after telling people that he'd buried the money somewhere among the granite boulders in the City of Rocks.

These granite boulders did not bring to mind cities, but they did remind me of Joshua Tree National Monument in California where similar outcrops of granite can be found. Bouldering and rock climbing are popular at Joshua Tree and perhaps not surprisingly, climbers converge on City of Rocks to test their mettle against bare rock. The unusual rock formations are the result of differential weathering. A hard granite cap covers softer stone, so that decomposition occurs more readily along the sides and bottom of these rocks than on top. In addition, rain enters cracks in the boulders and freezes, slowly breaking apart the rock.

In 1964 this site was selected as a National Historic Landmark and later recommended by the National Park Service for National Monument status. The proposal never got off the ground when local ranchers learned that cattle grazing would be curtailed on the public lands. Opposition arose when the federal government also proposed enlarging the site by acquiring private property by eminent domain.

The southern slopes of the Albion Range are the most northerly range extension for pinyon pine. The tree produces a large, nutritious nut, similar in size to a shelled peanut. In good nut years, Paiute and Shoshone Indians gathered in

Snake River, it's not surprising that salmon once spawned in Rock Creek and perhaps a few other streams in the range, but construction of dams on the Snake has eliminated these runs.

Although the people of Twin Falls may think of the Cassia Mountains as hills, they don't refer to the Albion Range as "hills." The Albion contains Cache Peak, at 10,339′ the highest peak in Idaho south of the Snake River. Several high summits including Big Bertha Dome (also known as Mt. Harrison), City of Rocks Dome as well as Cache Peak were glaciated and cirques, tarn lakes and moraines are

common. From the south they present a massive, hulking profile that is truly more impressive than one might expect from noting their seemingly small size on a map. Some 26,000 acres surrounding Cache Peak are included in southern Idaho's only proposed wilderness. For the most part, the area exhibits the high, rocky, scenic country, little good for any other exploitative use, that typifies most wilderness proposals.

On the southern fringes of this range is a granitic outcrop imaginatively called the City of Rocks. Some of the formations bear colorful

large groups to harvest the nuts, which provided a rich source of protein for the winter months. It was during these relatively brief periods of concentrated food excesses when Shoshone and Paiute groups could enlarge beyond the small family units that characterized their social organization. During most of the year, they had to travel widely to secure sufficient food to feed their families. As such, these gatherings were important for cementing family ties, socializing and trading.

Humans were not the only animal to utilize pinyon pine nuts. Grizzly bears eagerly sought the nuts to add needed fat layers before retiring into hibernation. Some birds, like the pinyon jay, rely almost exclusively upon pinyon nuts as a source of food. The resulting congregation of humans and wildlife at the pinyon forests must have made for an occasional surprise encounter, particularly between grizzlies and people.

Just east of the Albion Range is the Black Pine Range. A small range seen from Interstate 84 by Snowville, this one appears to be a single large hump rising out of the sage-covered slopes around it. From 9,385' Black Pine, the highest peak, other ridges nearly as high radiate. These peaks have been glaciated, but not nearly so extensively as the nearby Albion. However, there are other reminders of the Ice Age on the southeast side of the range, where old shorelines of glacial lake Bonneville can be seen. This lake, of which the Great Salt Lake is but a small remnant, once covered most of western Utah with several fingers lapped northward into Idaho. Although this range is predominantly sandstones and limestones, sedimentary rocks not conducive to mineral concentration, there were nevertheless some small gold and silver strikes and attendant mining camps.

In historical times, the Black Pine Range marked the western edge of bison distribution in Idaho, although occasional wandering herds were found even farther west. Antelope were also very plentiful in the area. Today, the bison are gone and the antelope herd is a fraction of its former size. At one time, sharp-

Hartley Canyon in the Sublette Range, which was named for trapper William Sublette, one of the founders of the Rocky Mountain Fur Company. STEPHEN TRIMBLE

tail grouse also were very common on the grasslands of the Black Pine, but overgrazing has eliminated most of their prime habitat and they exist in very small numbers.

The Sublette Range and Deep Creek Mountains are both east of Interstate 84. Both are similar geologically in that they consist of sedimentary sandstones and limestones with little surface drainage. Neither was glaciated and the highest peak, Deep Creek Peak, is only 8,670' in elevation. The gentle lower slopes are covered with grass and sage and the higher elevations have patches of aspen, Douglas fir and other conifers. They are not part of the National Forest system, but instead managed by the BLM. The Sublette Range was named for William Sublette, one of the better-known mountain men of the fur era, who helped to organize the Rocky Mountain Fur Company.

Within the Basin and Range province there are other smaller sub-ranges, such as the Jim Sage Mountains, Grouse Creek Mountains and others, most of which consist of a single ridge separating a drainage from one of the larger mountain masses. Taken as a whole, this region is very likely the least known of Idaho's mountain areas. Isolated like islands in a sea of sagebrush, they are nobody's destination as people race by heading toward the more dramatic Sawtooth or the cool lake country of northern Idaho, yet the vastness of the valleys coupled with the inviting, open ridges, make these Idaho mountains a region I intend to visit again.

12

OWYHEE MOUNTAINS

Aspen grove in the gently rolling Owyhee Mountains on a November morning. Lack of young aspen results from fire suppression and overgrazing by livestock. GEORGE WUERTHNER

In the extreme southwest corner of Idaho, bordering Nevada and Oregon, is Owyhee County—the most remote and unpopulated area of the state, with an average of 0.75 persons per square mile. At 5 million acres, Owyhee County is the second largest in the state, and larger than its namesake—the Hawaiian Islands.

The name Owyhee was the original spelling for the residents of the Hawaiian Islands. In 1818 several Hawaiians who had been employed as sailors jumped ship in Oregon and signed on as trappers with Donald MacKenzie of the Northwest Fur Company. Three of these Owyhees, as they were called, left MacKenzie's party to trap in the mountains southwest of Boise and never returned. MacKenzie named the mountains after them.

On a clear day looking southwest across the Snake River Plain from Boise, one can see the bold uplands of the Owyhee Mountains. Several peaks, including War Eagle Peak (8,051'), South Mountain (7,850'), and Quicksilver Mountain (7,994') are over 7,000' in elevation. Volcanic flows cap the Owyhees and these have been stripped by erosion to expose approximately 50 square miles of granite on War Eagle Mountain. Granite is also exposed on Whisky Mountain and Wilson Peak. South Mountain, as its name implies, lies south of the main range, but forms a prominent ridge. Outside of these granite uplifts, the remainder of the range is primarily basalt similar to the Snake River Plain, but of an older age. In general these mountains are rolling, with little relief; much of the range is like a gently tilting plateau slashed by deep rivers such as the Owyhee, Big and Little Jacks Creek, Battle Creek and others.

The aridity of the region is undisputed; the

The Owyhee River drains most of the western flank of the Owyhee Mountains, cutting a deep canyon through the overlying basalt. GEORGE WUERTHNER

locals joke that in the Owyhee country even the jackrabbits carry canteens. The lower elevations which once were carpeted with luxuriant bunchgrasses are today dominated by sagebrush and cheatgrass. Higher up, mountain mahogany and western juniper are found, with a few scattered stands of Douglas fir, subalpine fir and aspen growing on the cool north slopes. The Owyhee are apparently too isolated from other mountains ranges for lodgepole, ponderosa pine, or limber pine to have colonized them.

The Owyhee were home to wandering bands of Shoshone and Paiute Indians. These desert-dwelling peoples hunted antelope and bighorn, and gathered seeds and insects. But the Owyhee had something more to offer these bare-bones subsistence hunters than most of the sur-

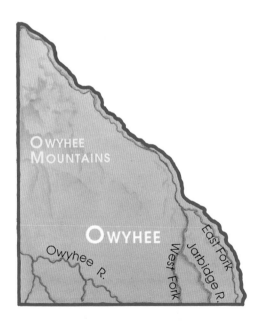

California bighorn sheep amid clumps of bluebunch wheatgrass, a plant that lives 50 to 100 years.
TED WEIGOLD

rounding ranges in the Great Basin: until the advent of dams, salmon spawned in many of the Owyhee streams and rivers. These salmon runs were extremely important to the Shoshones and the Paiutes, because they provided times when food resources were plentiful and concentrated enough to allow large congregations of family groups. This was when news was exchanged and potential lovers met, when old people exchanged stories and young children could play with others of their own age. For the rest of the year the Shoshones lived in scattered bands.

Although the Hawaiian trappers may have disappeared from the Owyhee, the wide-ranging fur brigades did not overlook the country. In 1826 Peter Skene Ogden, leading an expedition for the Hudson's Bay Company, trapped the headwaters of Big and Little Jacks Creek. Ogden wrote, "A more beautiful country I have not seen in this country. Certainly a fine variety of flowers, many known and many unknown. To me a strange sight to see red clover in abundance... a botanist would have had full employment and probably would have many additions to his stock."

After the trappers, miners entered the region. In 1863, Michael Jordan and 29 other prospectors left diggings in the Boise Basin to explore the possibilities of the Owyhee. Near Silver City on Jordan Creek they found placers subsequently traced to lode deposits on War Eagle Mountain. The miners soon discovered these lodes had more silver than gold. Processing of the ore began in 1864 and by 1866 the mines were producing $70,000 worth of metals a week. Eventually some $40 million in minerals was extracted.

After the mineral discoveries, range cattle were brought to the Owyhee. At one time more cattle and sheep were shipped from Murphy on the north edge of the Owyhee than from any other point in the U.S. As many as 100,000 longhorns roamed the open range. An early historian reported, "The summer range for cattle is almost inexhaustible, every hillside furnishing a luxuriant growth of bunch grass." Unfortunately, the grasses were exhaustible, as

was the wildlife which the early settlers indiscriminantly hunted. This type of thoughtless plunder is exemplified by a news item in the turn-of-the-century *Owyhee Nugget.* Two local men and their families reported killing on a two-day hunting trip: 45 deer, 3 sheep, 7 antelopes, 147 grouse, 1 badger, 9 mallard ducks, 6 doves and 1 rabbit. They somehow also had the time to catch 200 fish as well.

Today in the Owyhee Mountains, luxuriant growth of bluebunch wheatgrass as described by early settlers is merely a memory. One can find the grass surviving in cracks between rocks, beneath clumps of sagebrush, clinging to the sides of cliffs—any place a cow couldn't get at it. The effects of this extensive overgrazing, which is by no means limited to the Owyhee, but prevalent over much of the West, has wide-reaching implications.

For example, although bison probably never ranged this far west, antelope and bighorn sheep were once very abundant; in fact bighorns were more numerous than deer. By the 1920s the bighorn were exterminated by overhunting and competition with domestic livestock. Antelope declined to severely low numbers but hung on. On the other hand, deer probably increased somewhat after the first cattle arrived because the cows ate the grasses and encouraged the growth of shrubs—food deer prefer. But as the grasses continued to disappear, cattle increasingly had to browse important deer forage such as bitterbrush and mountain mahogany. Eventually even the deer herds declined.

Today nearly all of the Owyhee, which are managed by the Bureau of Land Management, are overgrazed by livestock, so that wildlife populations lose out in the competition for limited food resources. For example, a 1977-78 BLM survey indicated that 93 percent of the mule deer range habitat was in poor or fair condition. (Antelope range was in a similar condition.) According to the BLM report, the range cannot support deer in hard winters: many deer starve. Cattle, on the other hand, spend their winters at the home ranch getting fed supplemental hay. They go back on the ranges the following

The Owyhee Mountains' 8,000' elevation, as seen from the 2,000'-high Snake River plain. GEORGE WUERTHNER

year and give the plants no respite. On most public lands, livestock are allotted the vast majority of available forage (measured as AUM's or Animal Unit Months) with wildlife having to make its way with whatever is left over. The BLM has been ineffective in protecting the rangelands under its jurisdiction, but in fairness it should be mentioned that ranchers using their powerful political connections in Washington have prevented the agency from making any substantial livestock reductions.

The impact of domestic livestock on range-lands can be appreciated by comparing the range condition of this deer habitat (which livestock graze heavily) with bighorn habitat, which is only lightly touched by cows or domestic sheep. Some 69 percent of the Owyhee bighorn habitat is in good to excellent range condition and only five percent is in poor condition, even though the grass species, precipitation, and other physical factors on the big-horn ranges are often identical to those areas occupied by antelope and deer. The only difference is that the Owyhee bighorns live beyond where domestic livestock can graze, where the land is too steep or water is inaccessible.

On the east slope of the Owyhee Mountains lies the Jacks Creek plateau, where a remnant of the bunchgrass habitat still exists. The plateau has no permanent water supply and hence has been only lightly grazed. While over 75 percent of the Idaho BLM rangelands are in fair to poor condition and only 1.5 percent of the native rangelands are in excellent condition, well over three fourths of this nearly pristine

91

Livestock compete directly with wildlife for precious forage in the arid Owyhees. Overgrazing already has resulted in stream erosion and loss of habitat. JAMES K. MORGAN

grassland is found on the Jacks Creek Plateau. Over 100,000 acres of this plateau are still covered with lush native grasses—a biological relict. Here bluebunch wheatgrass grows in thick, continuous carpets as the early accounts of the Owyhee Country described.

But even the Jacks Creek Plateau soon may be grazed. Under pressure from local ranchers (with Washington's support), the BLM has proposed to build a 26-mile pipeline that would bring water to the plateau and open it to 4,000 cattle. As is frequently the case with many range improvements, the construction costs are borne by all taxpayers, although the benefits accrue to a few individuals. In the case of Jacks Creek, the pipeline will cost more than $150,000 to construct. Grazing fees from per-

mittees using the area will bring in $600 a year! Taxpayers will absorb the difference.

There is a further cost. In 1967 the Idaho Fish and Game introduced 12 California bighorns to the Jacks Creek drainage and by 1983 at least 15 bighorns roamed there. Should cattle be introduced onto the Jacks Creek Plateau, a large, nearly pristine bluebunch wheatgrass ecosystem will be lost and, in addition, the bighorns (which feed primarily on grasses) will be directly competing with cattle for forage.

Cattle overgrazing has other consequences for the Owyhee. In this arid land, all life gravitates toward riparian zones. The shrubs and trees provide nesting habitat for birds; other wildlife species utilize this vegetation for shade, escape cover, and thermal cover from

cold winter winds. Additionally, riparian zones contain important plant food for a host of animals. Of course, cattle also find riparian zones desirable and along many streams the impact from trampling, bank collapse, and heavy foraging has had serious effects upon wildlife.

For example, beaver are found in limited numbers in all the major streams and rivers of the Owyhee. They once were more numerous, but their primary food species—cottonwood, aspen and willow—have all but disappeared from these mountains. The cottonwood, in particular, has been hard hit. One can still find old homesteaders' cabins constructed from cottonwood, and at Three Fork of the Owyhee there is an ancient log jam composed primarily of cottonwood logs. But search long and hard, and you would be fortunate indeed to find a single living cottonwood in the Owyhee today. If cut, cottonwood quickly resprouts, but cattle relish young cottonwood shoots and where livestock grazing occurs in riparian zones all the new growth is eaten. Only one lone cottonwood is known to grow in the entire mountain range. It lives out its days in a remote, inaccessible portion of the Deep Creek canyon, a place where both the early settlers and their cattle could not reach.

With cottonwood gone and beaver in low numbers, river otters—who depend upon beaver to construct the bankside burrows they use as dens—also declined. The otters also were hurt by the increased erosion of streambanks caused by the trampling, loss of riparian vegetation, and sedimentation from the run-off of overgrazed ranges, because all these result in a decline of fish populations. Fish is the major food item in the otter's diet.

The loss of cottonwood and aspen has other ecological ramifications. These trees provided homes for cavity-nesting birds like flickers, owls and bluebirds, and their populations declined along with the beaver and otter.

BLM biologists estimate that 36 percent of the Owyhee riparian/meadow habitat is severely impacted by livestock use. Ninety percent of these areas exhibit lower vegetation diversity, limited tree and shrub cover and a high occurrence of undesirable weedy species compared with unimpacted streams!

The Owyhee support populations of the red-banded trout—a unique sub-species of rainbow trout that is specially adapted to high water temperatures. Red-banded trout may be a genetic relict. Scientists believe that all native trout east of the Cascades may have descended from ancient red-band stock. If this is true, the fish may hold the key to future improvements in the genetic diversity of hatchery-reared fish. Most red-banded trout live in tiny streams and while few ever grow larger than eight inches, they are abundant. I remember once hiking up Little Jacks Creek and driving schools of 100 or more of these trout in front of me. But overgrazing threatens these natives, just as it adversely affects salmon and steelhead along the head-waters of the Salmon, or cutthroat trout in southeastern Idaho's mountains.

These changes in the health of the land, its ecological productivity and its natural beauty may seem a concern only for nature lovers. What difference should it make to a city dweller if there are fewer beavers or cotton-woods in the Owyhee Mountains? The answer, in short, is: a lot. Without trees to hold the bank together increased erosion leads to faster run-off, greater channelization, and more destructive flooding. The loss of beaver dams that previously checked water flow necessitates human construction of large flood-control structures. All taxpayers must pay for dam construction to rectify a problem created by a few individuals and their animals.

The decrease in range quality as a result of overgrazing is undesirable for livestock as well as wildlife. It means that the nutritional quality of the range is lower and animals gain less weight. The fact that ranchers still can eke out a living is no indication that all is fine and dandy out on the back forty. Much of the western range is simply too arid for long-term profitable livestock production. You can raise more beef on an acre in humid Vermont than 100

Basalt (as here in the Squaw Creek drainage) dominates the Owyhees, although the highest peaks have exploded granite. Along the contact point between granite and overlying rocks, mineralization occurs; the silver mines at the headwaters of Jordan Creek were once the richest in the world. GEORGE WUERTHNER

acres in the Owyhee; Florida produces more beef than all the western states put together! Much of the land currently grazed can sustain long-term use only with drastically reduced livestock pasturage. Unfortunately most ranchers, with rising costs, lower range productivity and a general decline in demand for meat, can little afford to cut back on their herds—even if the long-term health of the land and their business requires it. For many, worrying about the range condition 20 years from now seems unimportant when they are struggling to keep the bank from foreclosing on their operations next month.

The Owyhee is an isolated and lonely land—a true wilderness—where a person can get lost and have a better-than-average chance of never being found. Last fall during the hunting season—a time when use is heaviest—I drove the main dirt road across the southern edge of the Owyhee and saw only three vehicles in two and a half days. In many ways, these mountains are wilder than much of Alaska or even the more spectacular mountainous areas of Idaho. However, even though one could walk for days in the Owyhee and never encounter another person, it's doubtful you would go that long without seeing a cow.

More than in any other part of Idaho, the mountains of the western fringe are dominated by big, brawling rivers. The Snake, Salmon, Payette, Boise, Secesh, and other streams have sliced deep canyons into the hard rocks of the granitic Idaho Batholith and basalts of the Columbia Plateau volcanics. These rivers define where ranges begin and end; the Seven Devils are sandwiched between the Salmon and Snake, the Boise Mountains are delineated by the valleys of the Payette and Boise Rivers, the Payette Crest lies between the North Fork of the Payette and South Fork of the Salmon.

The mountain ranges of the western fringe— the Soldier Mountains, Seven Devils, Boise Mountains, West Mountain, and the high country of the Boise Basin and Payette Crest— are, for the most part, lower in elevation than other mountains of the state. Except for the West Mountains between Round Valley and Long Valley, most of these ranges are separated by the narrow defiles of river canyons, with ridges and peaks that merge and plunge into a confused jumble making it difficult to determine where one range ends and the next begins. The higher elevations have been glaciated and cirques are abundant, but glacial ice did not override entire mountain ranges as in northern Idaho, and much of the low country displays the effects of water, rather than glacial, erosion.

Massive, old ponderosa pine with an understory of bluebunch wheatgrass and Idaho fescue, cloak the lower slopes. The mountains of the western fringe sustain a timber industry second only to that of northern Idaho in terms of board-feet cut each year. At higher elevations the ponderosa loses its dominance to forests of Douglas fir, lodgepole pine, limber pine, whitebark pine, subalpine fir and Engelmann spruce, while two other species—grand fir and western larch—reach their southern limits near

Ponderosa pine along the Middle Fork of the Boise River seem to grow out of pure granite. The Boise Mountains are generally rolling, with deep river canyons carved into their flanks. GEORGE WUERTHNER

An old homestead in Long Valley, with the West Mountains beyond. The Wests, which lie between the Payette and Weiser river valleys, have been extensively logged. GEORGE WUERTHNER

McCall. Although trees will sometimes grow right to the valley bottoms, especially in the higher mountains, in many places the lowest elevations tend to be open and dominated by shrubs and grasses.

As elsewhere in the west, the distribution and abundance of sagebrush and non-native plant species such as cheatgrass have increased dramatically as a result of the overgrazing. One early sheepman describing the Boise Mountains said: "All the range in the early days was good. The lower country, where there is now little but cheatgrass, was covered with bunchgrass, which served as dry feed throughout the winter."

Another early settler of the Boise region,

remarking on the changes that came to the land, said: "In Emmett Valley there was no sagebrush on the bench or the hills adjoining. In early and middle summer, the country would be covered with a dense stand of grass 12 to 18 inches high and resembled a wheat field. The settlers called it 'June Grass' because it matured in the month of June. It probably was one of the many species of brome grasses that are native to this locality. When the wind swept across the grass fields, the changing colors were beautiful to behold." Unfortunately such fields of native grasses are rare today and many of the lower mountain areas are barren or nearly so, with the eroding soil choking streams and reservoirs.

The fauna has changed as well. Most of the

95

Ponderosa pine, such as this massive one along the South Fork of the Payette River, were subject to timber harvest along many lower-elevation mountains of the western fringe. The area is Idaho's second largest timber producer after northern Idaho. GEORGE WUERTHNER

rivers draining these mountains, including the Boise, Weiser, Payette and other tributaries of the Snake, had salmon. The Shoshone and other Indian tribes used to congregate at these streams in summer to harvest the annual fish runs. Dams, sedimentation of spawning streams from logging, over-fishing, and loss of riparian zones from grazing, have all had their impacts and few rivers within this region today support salmon fisheries.

The rivers also attracted the trappers, who desired not fish, but furs. Many brigades wandered through the region, which once supported large beaver populations. The fur trappers put the first European names on the land and waterways. Boise means "wooded" in French and the Boise River was no doubt named by French Canadian trappers traveling with the early Northwest Fur Company brigades. Two members of Donald MacKenzie's 1818 trapping expedition were Francois Payette and Jack Weiser, whose names now identify a lake and two rivers of the region.

The early fur trappers travelled in brigades resembling small communities and were not the solitary trappers pictured in popular literature. For example, Alexander Ross led a trapping party along the Boise, Payette, and Weiser Rivers in 1824. With Ross were 55 men, 25 women, and 64 children. They had 392 horses and 212 beaver traps. Not only did they trap the entire Boise River to its mouth, but also they explored the Weiser and Payette Rivers and eventually returned to their headquarters at Flathead House in Montana with 5,000 beaver pelts from their year-long sojourn.

In 1834, Fort Boise was built as a supply post for the fur trade; Francois Payette was the first manager. The fort continued to function as an important supply point along the Oregon Trail even after the fur trade ended around 1840, but no other settlement occurred until the discovery of gold along the Boise and other rivers. Some of the earliest mining camps were Rocky Bar (1863), Atlanta (1864) and Idaho City, which by 1863 had a population of 6,267 and surpassed Portland as the largest city in the northwest.

The market provided by the mining camps stimulated the early livestock industry of the state and by the 1880s settlers began to ranch the higher mountain pastures, like those in Long Valley by Cascade. As elsewhere, many range wars were fought between established settlers and newcomers who wanted a piece of the free, open, public rangelands. The settlers of Long Valley posted guards at the Lardo Bridge and Smith's Ferry each spring to prevent outsiders from grazing their livestock in the area. Although they kept others from entering Long Valley, most of the surrounding mountain ranges were free for the taking. In some areas, the larger sheep outfits of the period had more than 20,000 animals.

Timber harvest on a large scale began fairly early in the region and one of the first corporations in the area was the Barber Lumber Company, which bought 25,000 acres of timberland along Grimes and Mores creeks in 1902. Other logging companies, including Payette Lumber, followed and logging the region's large old ponderosa pine soon became big industry. The Boise-Cascade Company was formed by the merger of the Barber and the Payette lumber companies in 1957.

Logging is still a major industry in the region. Many towns have small mills and some, like Horseshoe Bend, depend almost totally on the timber industry for their existence; other former mill towns, such as McCall, New Meadows and Riggins increasingly rely upon tourism. As in northern Idaho, the growing real estate business is stippling the larger valleys and hillsides with subdivisions. With a ready market in Boise, weekend cabin sites are a lucrative venture.

The most distinctive mountain range in the region is along the Idaho-Oregon border, where the 9,000' Seven Devils Mountains tower above the Snake River. The range and uplands are approximately 50 miles north to south and 25 miles across at the southern end, while only nine miles separate the Salmon River from the Snake River at the north end. The highest peaks are He Devil (9,393') and She Devil

LOGGING ROADS AND
DEFICIT TIMBER SALES

As the low-elevation, more productive timber stands have been harvested, the Forest Service and the wood products industry have turned increasingly to the remote, higher, steeper, lower-productivity forest sites to maintain mill timber supplies. The environmental costs of this policy have been great: increased erosion and sedimentation of rivers and creeks from roads, loss of wildlife security cover (hence a decline in usable wildlife habitat), earlier and more rapid run-off that increases spring flooding and reduces late summer water flows critical to both fisheries and irrigation, and finally, the loss of potential wilderness. In addition to these environmental costs, many of which are not considered in computations about the cost/benefit of timber sales, it has become increasingly expensive to get the logs out of the woods.

For example, it often costs more than $100,000 to build a mile of road in steep mountain topography and on many western national forests the cost of road building, timber sale preparation and administration greatly exceeds the receipts from timber sales. During the past six years every national forest in Idaho lost money on its timber sale program, and for many the losses were substantial. The Sawtooth, Targhee and Salmon recovered only 10 cents, and the Challis Forest 11 cents, for every dollar spent on their timber programs. More productive forests like the Clearwater managed to bring in only 26 cents for each dollar spent.

On many national forests, thousands of miles of costly new roads will be built during the next 10 to 50 years. The Clearwater National Forest, for example, presently has 4,200 miles of logging roads and plans to construct another 4,880 miles of new roads in the coming decades. At today's prices, the total construction cost of these new roads will exceed $400 million on this forest alone! The road density on the part of the Clearwater Forest managed for timber harvest then will average 5.8 miles of road per square mile of land, which obviously does not leave much room for elk, bear, and other large mammals to roam undisturbed by human contact or activity. In many areas the Forest Service proposes what it calls "advanced roading." These roads will be built into roadless areas to service timber harvest that will not be developed for decades into the future. Many conservationists feel advanced roading is just a mechanism to eliminate undesignated roadless areas from ever being considered for wilderness classification.

The Forest Service defends its deficit timber sales by ascribing benefits other than timber extraction to logging roads. Some people road-hunt, it says, hence claiming recreation is one benefit of these roads. It also justifies deficit timber sales as necessary for the economic stability of many small Idaho communities.

Forest Service critics point out that they are not opposed to timber harvest in general as long as it can be accomplished without severely jeopardizing other forest resources such as wildlife, watershed, soils, recreation and livestock grazing range. But, these critics say, deficit sales are a form of welfare that benefits the timber industry frequently at the expense of these other forest resources equally important to the national interest. In addition, they claim, subsidizing timber harvest on the less productive national forest lands makes it difficult for private owners to make a profit from their timberlands, thus thwarting incentives to reforest and intensively manage the generally highly productive private holdings.

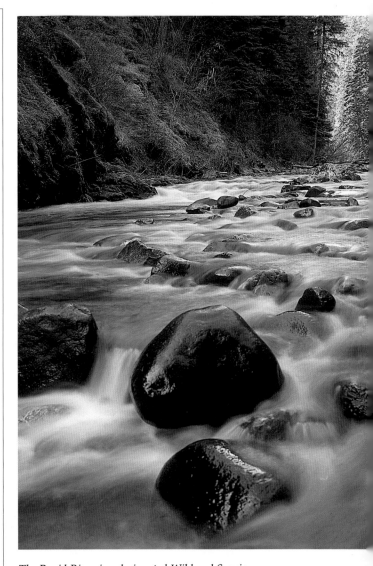

The Rapid River is a designated Wild and Scenic River flowing out of the Seven Devils Mountains. The pure water provides spawning habitat for chinook salmon and steelhead. Despite the Rapid River's Wild and Scenic status, its headwaters are open to logging. Conservationists propose wilderness status for the entire drainage to protect the river's fisheries. GEORGE WUERTHNER

The highest peaks of the Seven Devils have been glaciated and are part of the Hells Canyon National Recreation Area. D. WILDER

(9,387'), with a number of other peaks averaging around 9,000'. The massif of the Seven Devils is composed of volcanic tuffs and andesitic flows. In addition there are thick beds of limestone; White Monument is a ridge composed of marble (metamorphosed limestone). Outcrops of granite that lie exposed in the heads of Deep Creek, Indian Creek and Boulder Creek suggest that the entire mountain block is underlain by granite, but erosion has yet to expose it.

The Seven Devils were heavily glaciated above the 7,000' level. Cirque basins holding lakes and tarns abound around all the high peaks; the headwaters of several creeks and rivers such as the Lake Fork of the Rapid River, have U-shaped valleys.

Rich copper deposits in the Seven Devils led to the construction of the Kleinschmidt Grade for transporting ore from the mines to the Snake River by Homestead, Oregon. From there the ore was to be loaded on boats and carried to a railhead in Oregon. By the time the road was completed, a depression in the 1890s made further development of the mine impractical and the Grade was never used for its original purpose. Today the road provides access to the high country adjacent to the Seven Devils area.

Nearly all of the Snake River canyon and the adjoining mountains are part of the 652,488-acre Hells Canyon National Recreation Area created in 1975. A large part of this NRA lies in Oregon, but the high Seven Devils area of Idaho is included. The Seven Devils also are part of the 190,000-acre Hells Canyon Wilderness.

The Seven Devils are bounded on the west by the 75-mile-long Snake River Canyon which is, at nearly 8,000' deep, the deepest gorge in North America. (For comparison, the highest point on the Grand Canyon's rim is 5,630' above the Colorado River.) Over 67 miles of the river have been designated a Wild and Scenic River. The widely roaming Donald MacKenzie of the Northwest Fur Company probably was the first white man to traverse the canyon, pulling and rowing a boat from the Lewiston area all the way through it. MacKenzie concluded that river passage was possible, but recommended that land travel around the Wallowa Mountains would be easier. Today trails on both sides of the canyon follow the river and, because of its low elevation, provide fine early-season hikng possibilities.

Flowing off the eastern slope of the Seven Devils is the Rapid River, a clear mountain stream that still supports runs of chinook salmon and steelhead. A hatchery constructed at the mouth of the river augments natural runs. Twenty-six miles of the Rapid River have been given Wild and Scenic designation primarily to protect salmon and steelhead spawning habitat. The country surrounding its head-waters is roadless and conservationists propose wilderness designation for 33,000 acres.

Providing a scenic backdrop along the western edge of Long Valley between McCall and Cascade, the West Mountains separate the drainages of the Payette River and the Weiser River to the west. The West Mountains are a narrow, granite ridge, relatively low, rising only a few thousand feet above the surrounding high valleys. The highest peak, Council Mountain, is just over 8,000' in elevation.

The large, open Long Valley, some 30 miles in length and once a major summering ground for Boise area livestock, is now a summering ground for Boise residents. At the north end of Long Valley lies the town of McCall, which for 80 years was a major lumber producer, but today is one of the largest resort areas in the state. McCall, at 5,000', has the highest average annual snowfall (151") of any Idaho town, keeping the lifts operating at nearby Brundage Mountain Ski area in winter, while the cool forests of stately ponderosa pine and Douglas fir and the water recreation provided by Payette and upper Payette Lakes draws hoards of people each summer. During July and August weekends the hundred miles of road between Boise and McCall sometimes resemble a long, moving parking lot as thousands of people flee the heat of the Snake River Plain for the coolness of the mountains.

The abundant snowfall once fed glaciers that covered most of the high country to the north and east of Payette Lake. One can still see a large area of exposed white granite on the mountains across Payette Lake from McCall, where the glaciers scraped away the top soil leaving nothing for plants to root in. A large valley glacier flowed down the North Fork of the Payette to carve out the Payette Lake basin. The upper end of Long Valley is probably an outwash plain from this glacier. There are lateral moraines more than 500' high on the west side of the lake, indicating that the ice depth was considerably higher than the level of today's lake.

East and north of Payette Lake is a high plateau area sometimes referred to as the Payette Crest, which is a geological extension of the Salmon River Mountains. Rivers have carved deep canyons with steep slopes into the granites of these mountains. The headwaters of a number of rivers begin on the Crest including the Lake Fork, Secesh, South Fork of the Salmon, South Fork of the Payette and other rivers. The Payette Forest Plan recommends Wild and Scenic River designation for several of these streams, including the South Fork of the Salmon River, Secesh River and French Creek.

Except for the jagged granite spires of the Needles, the Payette Crest is not so rugged as the Sawtooths, nor does it rise abruptly from a valley as does the spectacular Lost River Range, yet the Crest has no shortage of steep slopes, heavily forested valleys and mountain lakes. A few of the peaks exceed 9,000', and 35 are over 8,000' in elevation.

Past logging on the unstable soils led to the destruction of the South Fork of the Salmon

Blackmare Lake along the Payette Crest east of McCall. The Payette Crest, separated from the Salmon River Mountains by the South Fork of the Salmon River, is an outcropping of the Idaho Batholith. TED WEIGOLD

Looking toward the Boise Mountains along the route of the Oregon Trail where the Boise Mountains meet the Snake River plain. TED WEIGOLD

River fisheries. This river once had a spawning run of 50,000 salmon a year; in recent years fewer than 300 have returned. In seeming disregard of this past watershed degradation, extensive new logging and roading is proposed. To protect the elk herds, fisheries and fragile soils of the Idaho Batholith sections of these mountains, a total of 555,000 acres—the majority of it along the Payette Crest and South Fork of the Salmon River, are proposed for wilderness designation by Idaho conservationists.

South of Idaho City are the Boise Mountains, also a southern continuation of the Idaho Batholith. Outlying grassy ridges of these mountains just beyond Boise's city limits form a backdrop for Idaho's largest city. These mountains, nearby rivers and several large reservoirs provide year-round outdoor recreation for Boise residents, making it one of the more desirable places to live in the western United States.

The Boise Mountains are for the most part steep-sided, with open, grass-covered south-facing slopes, and forested north slopes. Many of the lower-elevation areas still are used as winter, spring and fall ranges for livestock; in places such as the Middle Fork of the Boise River, overgrazing is rampant, the mountains are literally eroding away and once-lovely trout streams are now choked with sand and sediments.

The Boise Mountains, like others in this region, are primarily granite with basalt flows of the Snake River Plain along their lower valleys and southern margins. Rivers such as the Payette and Boise have gouged deep canyons into the otherwise rolling surface and its highest peaks include 9,451′ Trinity Mountain, 9,730′ Steel Mountain, and 9,368′ Bald Mountain.

North of Camas Prairie is a sub-range of the Boise Mountains called the Soldier Mountains. These are separated from the main Boise Mountains by the South Fork of the Boise River. The highest peaks include the 10,095′ Smoky Dome and 9,694′ Iron Mountain. In this area, the naturalist John Townsend wrote that, during his 1834 passage along the base of the

Soldier Mountains to the South Fork of the Boise, his party found camas so abundant in Camas Prairie that they camped to gather the nutritious bulbs. In the South Fork of the Boise River, salmon were thick: "Towards evening, we descended to a fine large plain, and struck Boisee, or Big Wood river, on the borders of which we encamped. This is a beautiful stream, about one hundred yards in width, clear as crystal, and in some parts, probably twenty feet deep. It is literally crowded with salmon, which are springing from the water almost constantly."

These salmon fisheries were struck a debilitating blow by mining that generated great quantities of sediments. Both the Soldier and Boise mountains were the center of major mining activity during the 1800s. In 1862, George Grimes, Moses Splawn and a small group of prospectors found placer deposits on Grimes Creek. Soon thousands of miners were flooding into the Boise Basin. Many were making $8 to $20 a day and a few lucky ones scraped in more than $100 for a day's work. New discoveries followed at Placerville, Pioneerville, Centerville and Idaho City. In the fall of 1864 massive gold and silver lode deposits were found at Atlanta, where some mining activity continues today. Barren tailings piles are characteristic of mined areas and appear as low hills just south of the highway by Idaho City. The streambeds were torn up by gold dredges, beginning in 1898 and ending in 1952.

Despite the mining and logging that has occurred since the 1860s, several large chunks of roadless country remain. Wilderness advocates would like to see a number of areas protected as wilderness, including the 122,000-acre lake-studded Trinity Mountain area, the 20,000-acre Danskin-South Fork Boise River, the 90,000-acre Lime Creek area in the Soldier Mountains, and the 40,000-acre Breadwinner area just north of Trinity Mountain.

Wildlife here has recovered from low populations at the turn of the century. Over-hunting and habitat destruction by livestock are now prevented by stricter government control. But,

Fresh snow covers the Soldier Mountains, as seen from the Camas Prairie. This prairie was a favorite campsite for the Indians who dug camas roots, which grow in such profusion here as to color the ground blue when the blossoms are out. TED WEIGOLD

with few exceptions, far less wildlife wanders the western Idaho mountains today than did at the coming of the European. Some species, such as deer, are more common at higher elevations than in the past, but they are simply occupying habitat that once supported bighorn sheep, antelope or elk. Many species were wiped out and exist only because of extensive restocking programs. In 1909, 25 elk had to be transplanted from Yellowstone to the South Fork of the Payette River to re-establish elk in this region. Elk now are very abundant with more than 12,000 animals on the Payette Forest alone, but

increased timber harvest and roading threaten the future of these herds.

Unlike elk, which recovered well from initial reductions early in the century, bighorn sheep, once numerous in the headwaters of the Boise, Payette, and Salmon rivers, were eliminated by the 1920s. Mountain goats, because of their preference for isolated high country, fared better than sheep and can be found in the mountains lying in the upper drainages of the Middle and South Forks of the Boise River, South Fork of the Payette, and South Fork of the Salmon. One predator which, if it ever

recovered to former numbers, could have an impact on elk, deer, and other large ungulates, is the wolf. Wolves have been sighted on the Boise and Payette forests in recent years, particularly along the South Fork of the Salmon River, but no breeding pairs are known.

The mountains of the western fringe seem to have suffered the most of everything: placer mining, heavy grazing, logging, and now a recreation boom unparalleled in any other part of the state except perhaps for northern Idaho. In spite of all this, however, the western fringe remains largely wilderness.

101

Idaho's Named Peaks Above 10,000 Feet

Borah Mountain	Lost River Range	12,662
Leatherman Peak	Lost River Range	12,230
Diamond Peak	Lemhi Range	12,197
Hyndman Peak	Pioneer Mountains	12,078
Castle Peak	White Cloud Mountains	11,815
Ryan Peak	Boulder Mountains	11,795
Bell Mountain	Lemhi Range	11,612
Smiley Mountain	Pioneer Mountains	11,508
Scott Peak	Beaverhead Mountains	11,393
Black Dome	Pioneer Mountains	11,353
Invisible Mountain	Lost River Range	11,330
Shelly Mountain	White Knob Mountains	11,278
Galena Peak	Boulder Mountains	11,170
Dickey Peak	Lost River Range	11,141
Grouse Creek Mountain	Pahsimeroi Range	11,085
Standhope Peak	Pioneer Mountains	11,075
Flatiron Mountain	Lemhi Range	11,019
Lem Peak	Lemhi Range	10,985
May Mountain	Lemhi Range	10,971
Boulder Peak	Boulder Mountains	10,966
Massacre Mountain	Lost River Range	10,924
Sheep Mountain	Boulder Mountains	10,910
Saddle Mountain	Lost River Range	10,795
Copper Basin Knob	Pioneer Mountains	10,784
Baldy Mountain	Bitterroot Mountains	10,773
Bear Mountain	Lemhi Range	10,744
Sunset Peak	Lost River Range	10,693
Snowyside Peak	Sawtooth Mountains	10,651
Mogg Mountain	Lemhi Range	10,573
King Mountain	Lost River Range	10,500
Sheephorn Peak	Lemhi Range	10,465
Heart Mountain	Beaverhead Mountains	10,422
Twin Peaks	Salmon River Mountains	10,340
Cache Peak	Albion Range	10,335
Bald Mountain	Salmon River Mountains	10,313
Norton Peak	Boulder Mountains	10,285
Mackay Peak	White Knob Mountains	10,273
Parks Peak	Sawtooth Range	10,208
Smoky Dome	Soldier Mountains	10,095
Mount McGuire	Salmon River Mountains	10,082
Big Peak	Smoky Mountains	10,060
Porphyry Peak	White Knob Mountains	10,012

ACKNOWLEDGMENTS

I would like to thank Paul Link of Idaho state University for providing geological information on the mountains of southeast Idaho and Dave Alt of the University of Montana for reviewing the geology chapter. Maps and color illustrations © Karen Jacobsen, 1986. In addition, the library staffs of Idaho State University and the University of Montana were more than enthusiastic in helping me track down source material. I also wish to thank the various state and federal agencies that provided information, or answered questions, as I researched this book—in particular, Roger Rosentreter and Al Sands of the Boise BLM, and Tom Parker of the Idaho Fish and Game department. Rick Johnson of the Idaho Conservation League provided me with background on various Idaho wilderness proposals. There were many people whose names I never learned, like the Chamber of Commerce representative in Salmon or the Sawtooth NRA information officer in Twin Falls, as well as others who generously gave of their time and knowledge. Finally, a special thanks to Mollie Matteson, who reviewed portions of the manuscript and offered many editorial suggestions.

ABOUT THE AUTHOR

Based in Missoula, Montana, George Wuerthner has been employed as a university instructor in California, a surveyor in Wyoming, a guide and packer in Montana, a wilderness ranger in Alaska and a botanist in Idaho. Between jobs he has backpacked, skied, canoed and kayaked extensively in wild places, taking wilderness journeys of up to four months' duration. His writing and photography have appeared in *Arizona Highways, Natural History, Wilderness,* Reader's Digest books, *Audubon,* Sierra Club calendars, *California Magazine, Outdoor Life, Outside,* Alaska Geographics, *Montana Magazine* and elsewhere.

Opposite page: Sawtooth Mountains from Stanley Basin. WILLIAM H. MULLINS
Right: Author fishing in the Selway River.

SOURCES

The following are sources of maps and information about Idaho's mountains.

Idaho Fish and Game Department, 600 S. Walnut, Boise, ID 83707

Idaho Department of Parks and Recreation, Statehouse, Boise, ID 83720

Idaho Conservation League, Box 844, Boise, ID 83701

Idaho Department of Tourism, State Capitol, Boise, ID 83701

Wilderness Society, Idaho Field Office, 413 W. Idaho St., Boise, ID 83702

Greater Yellowstone Coalition, 40 E. Main, Bozeman, MT 59715

U.S. Geological Survey, Federal Center, Denver, CO 80225

Boise National Forest, 1750 Front St., Boise, ID 83702

Caribou National Forest, 2509 S. 4th Ave., Pocatello, ID 83201

Challis National Forest, Forest Service Building, Challis, ID 83226

Clearwater National Forest, Rt. 1, Orofino, CA 83544

Idaho Panhandle National Forest, 1201 Ironwood Dr., Coeur d'Alene, ID 83814

Nezperce National Forest, 319 E. Main St., Grangeville, ID 83530

Payette National Forest, Box 1026, McCall, ID 83638

Salmon National Forest, Forest Service Building, Salmon, ID 83467

Sawtooth National Forest, 1525 Addison Ave. East, Twin Falls, ID 83301

Targhee National Forest, 420 N. Bridge St., St. Anthony, ID 83445

Bureau of Land Management, State Office, P.O. Box 042, Boise, ID 83724

For the Owyhee Mountains, write: Bureau of Land Management, Boise District Office, 3948 Development Ave., Boise, ID 83705

Next in the
Idaho Geographic Series

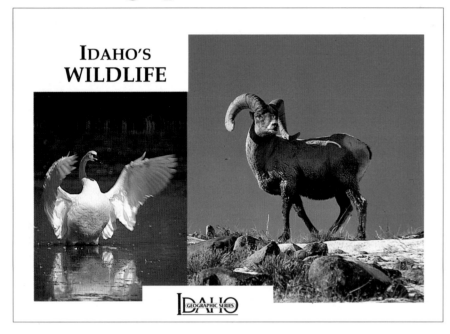

IDAHO'S WILDLIFE

Idaho harbors a cornucopia of wildlife species that makes a priceless heritage for the state. This book is the complete picture of the animals, their life histories, behaviors and habitat. Profusely illustrated, you'll see animals in action as in no other book on the subject. This volume tells about the conditions of wildlife as the first explorers saw them, how some of those populations changed and almost disappeared, and the story of their management today. From big game to birds of prey, from sport fish to reptiles, this is your guide to Idaho's fabled wildlife treasure.

ABOUT THE IDAHO GEOGRAPHIC SERIES

This series is your guide to enjoying and understanding Idaho's places, people and landscapes.

Color photography of the unspoiled country of Idaho illustrates every book, and each text is written especially for this series to help you explore, experience and learn about this fascinating state.

WRITE TO:
AMERICAN GEOGRAPHIC PUBLISHING
P.O. BOX 5630
HELENA, MT 59604
(406) 443-2842

Titles in production or planning are:

Idaho's Wildlife
Idaho's Desert Country
Idaho: A Portrait of the Land and Her People
Idaho's Rivers

Order early: Pre-publication discounts are available.

Please send us suggestions for titles you would like to see and your comments about what you see in this volume.